For my father,
LERONE BENNETT, SR.

For my publisher,
JOHN H. JOHNSON

CONTENTS

AUTHOR'S
PREFACE

In five essays organized around the general theme, *The Negro Mood,* I have attempted to dig beneath the surface and expose the psychic mechanisms of the Black Fury that is rolling across the land.

It is of encounter that I speak here—the encounter between man and man and mind and mind and the deeper, more problematical encounter of man—black man and white man—with himself. What I have attempted to do in these essays is to provide a new framework of understanding for a series of interlocking encounters that go to the heart of our meaning as a people.

The Negro rebellion is, in fact, four different rebellions: a rebellion against the conservative within and the conservative without; a rebellion on the streets and a rebellion on the thoroughfares of the mind. The four rebellions are analyzed and correlated in four chapters: "Mood," "Structure," "Ethos," "Passion." The fifth and final chapter, "Tea and Sympathy: Liberals and Other White Hopes," is a frank analysis of the limitations of our responses to the quadruple rebellion.

Four of these essays were written expressly for this book. "Voices from the Cave," however, is an expanded version of a lecture delivered at the University of Wisconsin in Milwaukee.

Throughout this book, I have discussed the Negro rebellion as a social fact with a social past. I have tried here to understand not Negroes, but rebellion, not segregation, but power. In this effort, I have used the traditional tools of social psychology and some of the concepts of modern existentialists, particularly the concept of the "boundary situation." This book is also informed by a study of the history of Negro revolt and resistance.

There is a regrettable tendency on the part of some Americans to discuss the current upheaval as an isolated event of the sixties. This is, as the title essay points out, a nursery-rhyme approach to the historical process. The Negro rebellion is an outgrowth of migration, urbanization, increasing self-consciousness, and increasing alienation. In order to make an adequate response to that rebellion, we must view it within the context of a long history of developing protest and social contention.

I have attempted, in the title essay, to lay bare the roots of the rebellion and the inarticulate premises that guide it. These premises, which will seem revolutionary to some, reflect the Negro situation (a situation defined by power or, rather, the lack of power) and the American situation (a situation defined by broken community).

The factor of power, which is central to an understanding of the Negro-white situation, is discussed at greater length in "Black Establishment," an

analysis of Negro decision makers and their interaction and lack of interaction with liberals and the
white power structure. This analysis, incidentally,
was written before the Harlem and Rochester riots
which illuminated the strains and stresses within the
Negro power structure.

Another factor of immense importance in the
current upheaval is the revolution in symbolism, the
revolution in meaning, the revolution of the Word.
The struggles on the streets are reflections of struggles in the minds of Negroes who are migrating in-
ternally. The revolution within—the quest for
identity on the part of men who are denied an
acceptable image of themselves by our unilaterally
subjective pattern of meaning—dominates the next
two sections, "Ethos" and "Passion."

The internal revolution, a revolution revolving
around the re-interpretation of the Negro past and
the Negro folk tradition is relevant, I think, to the
lives of all Americans. My primary concern here is
the abiding responsibility of free people to know
themselves. We are what we are today because of
what happened yesterday, and our todays will remain horrible for precisely as long as we avoid the
necessary confrontation with yesterday.

"Ethos" and "Passion" invoke the memory and
the meaning of the Negro past, which is also the
white man's past. Our current crisis calls us to a
remembrance of that past and to the large part
Negroes have played in the American experience. It
calls us, above all else, to a celebration of the
black-white roots in the subsoil of our lives.

The implications of all this are immense. The

Negro rebellion, as "Liberals and Other White Hopes" points out, is not really a Negro rebellion; it is an *American* rebellion and it is asking us searching questions about our lives.

Who are we?

What do we *really* believe?

What, precisely, is America?

Seen whole, within the context of forces contending for dominance, the Black Fury is a gift in disguise. It is an opportunity for re-evaluation and re-assessment. It is an opportunity for the creation of that America which has not yet been discovered.

This book was designed to provoke thought, concern, even anger. It is not, by any means, a final answer; but if it raises new questions it will have served its purpose.

I am indebted to many people: John H. Johnson, my publisher; Doris E. Saunders, director of the Johnson Publishing Company Book Division; Ida-rae Jackson, Ariel Strong, Herbert Temple, and Basil Phillips; Lucille Phinnie, research librarian; and John Britton and Lawrence Still who shared with me their experiences in covering key events of the rebellion. I am also indebted to my wife, Gloria, and my four children, Joy, Constance, Courtney, and Lerone III, for their patience and understanding. I alone am responsible for limitations of structure, articulation, and style.

Lerone Bennett, Jr.

August, 1964

If I am not for myself,
Who is for me?
If I am for myself alone,
What am I?
If not now,
When?

—HILLEL

The
NEGRO
MOOD

I
MOOD:
Project "C"

FEBRUARY, 1963, was a quiet, curious month.

It was the second month of the Emancipation centennial and men looked back, in hope and in anger, to Abraham Lincoln's words and Abraham Lincoln's deed.

John Fitzgerald Kennedy, the thirty-fifth President of the United States, and Medgar Evers, an obscure NAACP official, spoke in this month of that last full measure of devotion which both would pay before the year had run its course. In Birmingham, four children who would soon be dead heard Lincoln's name spoken and his deed praised. From a thousand pulpits and a thousand lecterns came words of hope and words of freedom. Centennial orators declaimed, proclamations were read, prayers were spoken. And all went on as before. Rats scampered across the littered corridors of Harlem tenements and water bubbled from the "white" and "colored" fountains in the Birmingham city hall. Papers of importance were signed as before. Black men stood in lines before unemployment offices, new plays opened on Broadway and schoolboys recited the Gettysburg Address.

It was a curious business in a curious month in a curious year—Negro and white Americans marching on to danger with the words and the deeds of Lincoln on their lips and in their minds. There were no signs then of the black fury to come. But there was a stillness in the Harlems of the mind and in Arlington the white crosses stood mute and accusing in the bright February sun.

In this quiet, eerie month, a tall, thin man slipped into Birmingham, Alabama. He arrived at midday on Flight 623, Delta Airlines, and went immediately to Gaston's Motel, the modernistic glass and brick pile in the heart of the Negro ghetto.

Before unpacking, the tall man opened a brown leather attaché case and extracted a sheaf of papers. The papers were marked CONFIDENTIAL. And across the top of each page was a legend:

PROJECT "C"

Project "C" was the code name for a proposed series of racial demonstrations in Birmingham.

And what did the "C" stand for?

It was a shorthand symbol for a chillingly blunt concept: CONFRONTATION. A confrontation between Negroes and whites—not in the courts but on the steps of city hall, not at the conference table but in the streets, not by ones and twos but by hundreds and thousands.

The man behind the concept was Martin Luther King, Jr., the thirty-four-year-old president of the Southern Christian Leadership Conference (SCLC). King had emerged from the Montgomery bus boycott as the spiritual leader of a passive resistance movement that changed the contours of race relations. In the first two years of the sixties, he attracted international attention with a series of direct action thrusts in Southern cities. But none of the thrusts led to a dramatic breakthrough. As the Emancipation Proclamation Centennial drew near, King cast about for a Bastille, i.e., a key point that could yield more than a local or symbolic victory. With incredible boldness, he selected Birmingham which was widely regarded as an impregnable fortress of Jim Crow.

The detailed plans for Project "C" were hammered out in a series of meetings at SCLC's Atlanta headquarters in the summer and fall of 1962. The dominant personalities in these meetings were King and three Baptist ministers: Ralph D. Abernathy, treasurer of SCLC; Wyatt Tee Walker, executive director of SCLC; Fred L. Shuttlesworth, secretary of SCLC and president of SCLC's Alabama affiliate.

Project "C" was scheduled and postponed several times. By February, 1963, however, King was convinced that a showdown situation was necessary for racial progress in Birmingham. There was no way for him to know then, there was no way, really, for anyone to know that the project prophetically called "C" would lead Negro and white Americans to the brink of an eyeball-to-eyeball confrontation.

It was decided early in February to proceed with Project "C" on April 3, the day after Birmingham's municipal election. But SCLC was nothing if not thorough. Two months before D-day, Wyatt Tee

Walker was dispatched to Birmingham to lay the formal foundations.

In Room 16 at Gaston's Motel, in the month of February, 1963, Walker, a tall Baptist minister in black horn-rimmed glasses and an Ivy League suit, sat for a long time studying the "battle plans." Then, as the sun dropped behind the hills, the Rev. Mr. Walker slipped out of his room and kept his first appointment.

By nightfall, the first stone was laid.

No one knew then that a revolution was in the offing.

February was a quiet month.

Rats scampered across the littered corridors of Harlem tenements and in Birmingham the statue of Vulcan on Red Mountain was aglow.

In the next few weeks, Walker, Shuttlesworth and other SCLC aides shuttled in and out of Birmingham, contacting key persons and laying the groundwork for the struggle to come. Secondary and tertiary targets were selected, and a code system was devised to confuse "the enemy." On the telephone SCLC aides spoke obliquely of "candidates" for the scheduled baptism.

Throughout this period, strategic plans were reviewed and refined. The best routes for mass marches were plotted and listed on a map. SCLC aides walked from the Sixteenth Street Baptist Church to city hall and noted the time on a chart. They also noted key features of the terrain and made cryptic notes on charts and pieces of paper.

All through the early months of 1963, while centennial orators postured and threatened, SCLC aides worked. Information on the ownership of business and industrial concerns in Birmingham was compiled; and wealthy whites and Negroes were lined up as potential contributors to a bail bond fund.

While these events were unfolding, local leaders made one final attempt to negotiate with Birmingham's white leaders. When this effort failed, Martin Luther King, Jr., and his top aides invaded the city and started Phase I of Project "C."

For more than a month, King and his nonviolent army struggled with the forces of Theophilus Eugene (Bull) Connor, the Birmingham commissioner of public safety. Thousands were arrested and humiliated amid scenes of incredible brutality. Some demonstrators were bitten by police dogs; others were bowled over by high-powered water hoses. The whole angry fabric of resistance and rebellion reached a peak on May 11-12, 1963, with a bombing counterattack by white segregationists. Angered by the bombings, Negroes rioted, burned the stores of white businessmen and fought with policemen, state troopers, and firemen.

The Bastille of Birmingham was a turning point in the Negro resistance movement. Sparks from the flames of Birmingham leaped from ghetto to ghetto, igniting inflammable material that had been gathering for years, welding Negroes into a great black mass of livid indignation.

Something snapped during the struggle in the streets of Birmingham. The billy clubs, the fire hoses and the contempt for Negro women and children swept away the last vestiges of credulity and millions knew themselves victims.

After Birmingham, the Negro Freedom Movement grew in intensity and scope. In 1963 alone, there were more than two thousand demonstrations (sleep-ins, sit-ins, pray-ins, wade-ins and mass marches) and more than ten thousand demonstrators were arrested.

As the year wore on, lurching to three bloody climaxes, the assassinations of President Kennedy and Medgar Evers and the bomb-murder of four children in a Birmingham church, resistance stiffened in the North. Organizations of white taxpayers, parents, and realtors came forward to agitate against open occupancy and open school enrollment. More and more people, as the year wore on, reminded the Negro of his situation: minority status maintained by the naked force of an overwhelming majority. As the North-South consensus developed, as the great tide of white concern in the North receded, Negro leaders found themselves far away from their accustomed haunts, swept up on the burning beaches of history in ridiculous poses. What did they do? Some proposed a strategic retreat to the old islands of protest and voter registration. But others, with remarkable boldness, struck out for new and higher ground.

Beginning in January, 1964, one hundred and one years after emancipation, the Freedom Movement began to inch toward the dangerous road of open and continuous self-assertion. The momentum began to build with smashing school boycotts in Northern cities, with mass confrontations in Maryland, Georgia, and Florida.

There was a new dimension in these demonstrations. The movement, before Birmingham, was largely confined to a small elite of nonviolent student professionals. In the summer of 1963, the angry men of World War II and the Korean War entered the ranks. And as 1964 began there was an involvement of the lowest strata of the Negro working class. The rent strikes of New York City and Washington and hunger marches in Chicago were reflections of the engagement of a hitherto uncommitted group.

Step by step, demonstration by demonstration, Negroes inched toward open and bitter alienation. They sprawled in the streets to stop traffic; they chained themselves to dump trucks to stop work at construction sites; they used their bodies to bar entrance to schools and boards of education.

A measure of the change in mood was the increasing harshness of Negro-white confrontations. In Maryland, Mississippi, Illinois, Florida, and New York, Negro and white Americans faced each other in 1964 in massive confrontations that resembled miniature wars.

By the summer of 1964, some of the more venturesome Negro leaders were openly calling for civil disobedience campaigns, i.e., the nonpayment of taxes, noncooperation with government agencies and massive attempts to create what Bayard Rustin, a leading philosopher of the movement, called "creative social confusion."

At the root of the current upheaval is a cataclysmic shift in the mood of Negroes, a shift mirrored in changing patterns of protest and social contention. The causes of this epochal shift lie deep in the total Negro-white situation. The current rebellion, which began in February, 1960, and reached a peak in 1963-64, cannot be understood apart from the long history of preparatory work. To focus on the peak years of 1963-64 and to ignore the long history of developing protest is to miss not only the mountain but the meaning of the peak.

Bryan Edwards, the great anatomist of social upheavals, said once that it takes at least three generations to make a revolution.

The first generation, in short, submits.

The second generation protests.

The third generation acts.

One does not have to accept Edwards' theory in its entirety to recognize the core of truth it contains. Revolutions do not spring full-blown from the head of Zeus or Martin Luther King, Jr. They are products of slowly accumulating changes in the nerve plasm of individuals. Over a long period of time, discontent builds up, accumulates and strains against the dams of social habit. The explosion that follows is a product of action and a lack of action, the increasing pressure of discontent as well as the counterpressure of the dam.

The dam against which Negro discontent is focused is white power. Any realistic analysis of the Negro rebellion must begin with the Negro's situation, a situation defined by power or the lack of it.

In the beginning, insofar as the Negro is concerned, was not a word but a monstrous fact: white power.

Forty-one years ago, a group of "prominent white citizens" of Tuskegee, Alabama, defined the Negro's situation in a frank talk with Robert R. Moton,

Booker T. Washington's successor as president of Tuskegee Institute. In the summer of the Negro's discontent, Mayor Allen Thompson of Jackson, Mississippi, used almost the same words in a frank talk to a group of Negro ministers. Here are the two quotes.

"You understand," the prominent white citizen said in 1923, "that we have the legislature, we make the laws, we have the judges, the sheriffs, the jails. We have the hardware stores and the arms."

"I'm not threatening you," Mayor Thompson said in the summer of 1963. "But we've got the guns, we've got the force."

Power.

Let us begin by talking about power.

White guns, white judges, white armies, white tanks, white bombs, white symbols: this is the element into which the Negro is flung and to which he must make a creative social response or die.

From birth to death, the Negro is handled, distorted and violated by the symbols and tentacles of white power, tentacles that worm their way into his neurons and invade the gray cells of his cortex. As he grows up, he makes a tentative adjustment to white power. At puberty, if he survives and if he remains outside prisons or insane asylums, he makes a separate peace—a peace of accommodation or protest. The price of this peace is high, fantastically high. The price, quite simply, is social emasculation. The Negro not only dons a mask; he becomes, in many instances, the mask he dons. Behind the public mask is a man who fears, cries, bleeds, loves, defecates, hates—a man who knows, as James Weldon Johnson knew, that "the resort to force remains and will doubtless remain the rightful recourse of oppressed peoples"—a man who knows this but rejects it, as Johnson rejected it, "because in our case it would be futile."

From a logical standpoint, of course, there can be only two basic responses to arbitrarily imposed power: open revolt or accommodation. The Negro resistance movement has moved within the confines of two contradictory imperatives: 1) the need to reject open revolt and 2) the need to reject acceptance. This is a cruel and grinding dilemma. If the Negro revolts, in other words, he loses all. But if he refuses to revolt, he also loses all. For acceptance, on whatever level, is violation.

The history of the Negro in America, then, has been a quest for a revolt that was not a revolt—a revolt, in other words, that did not seem to the white power structure to be an open revolt. Martin Luther King, Jr., and the sit-in students, as we shall see, solved the technical problems by clothing a resistance movement in the comforting garb of love and forgiveness.

Before King, almost all Negroes were enmeshed in different levels of collaboration. The overwhelming weight of the culture pushed them into "their places" and, as Ralph J. Bunche pointed out in the forties, all Negroes had "a place" in America and, in Chicago or Birmingham, they usually remained in it. Some Negroes, of course, accommodated themselves better than others. Some internalized the values of white people and imitated them. Still others adjusted to external factors and maintained—or tried to maintain—internal freedom. The latter group adjusted but protested every step of the way. But protest is not revolt. This is the point of departure for an understanding of the Negro rebellion. One sends a telegram protesting an indignity or one passes a resolution condemning it or one appeals to authority for help or protection or redress. The question of revolt arises when the request is denied and one comes hard up against the question: "What are you going to do about it?"

Faced with overwhelming power, backed up by the implacable hostility of a dominant majority, the Negro has elaborated four techniques of resistance: direct action, violent and nonviolent, black nationalism and protest, a vague, umbrella word covering a whole constellation of postures and poses revolving around litigation, lobbying and a propaganda of enlightenment. Distinct from and, in most cases, opposed to these strategies of contention is a strain of accommodation which reached its height —some would say its depth—in the submissive policy of Booker Taliaferro Washington.

The weaving and interweaving of three additional themes should also be noted: the search for an opening to the masses; the quest for the right key or instrument (ballots, bullets, Bibles, law books, dollar bills or the human body used as a weapon in strikes, boycotts, marches or other direct attacks); the quest for reliable allies (liberals or radicals, aristocrats or laborers). Hovering over all, subtly shaping and influencing all, is the harsh imperative of avoiding action that would unite all white Americans in a "holy war" against all Negro Americans.

The Negro situation spawns individual types who respond to white power with life styles corresponding to the four major techniques of resistance: militants, for example, who express themselves through protest; moderates who essay a middle course between accommodation and protest; accommodators who accept segregation and strive for various modes of individual advancement; and activists who repudiate protest, accommodation and moderation and demand action, violent or nonviolent. In a completely different category are Negro nationalists who say the civil rights struggle is useless and recommend total separation, either in America or Africa.

The dialogue of destiny in the ghetto is dominated by the militants and moderates who man the command posts of the institutions and associations of the black elite. But the hegemony of militants and moderates has never been complete. Since the thirties, there has been a continuing conversation between militants and moderates of the elite and activists and black nationalists.

The moderately militant black elite has scored impressive victories (the NAACP legal campaign and the Urban League welfare program), but it has not made an appreciable dent in the great white wall, a fact which does not, taken alone, condemn it. It may be—and only time will tell—that the wall is unbreachable. And yet it is difficult to avoid the conclusion that elite failures stem from self-imposed limitations of style and what Ralph J. Bunche called "a narrow vision of leadership."

The moderately militant black elite, from the very beginning, cut itself loose from the only element that could give it real power—the Negro masses. This was a fatal error that condemned the elite to impotence and the masses to apathy. Having forsworn mass action and risky adventures for freedom, having, in fact, committed themselves to the system, thereby losing freedom of action, elite members had, of necessity, to approach white men of power as suppliants who could not make serious threats and back them up.

Seconded by powerful voices in the white liberal establishment, tolerated and sometimes encouraged by the white power structure, the black elite created the protest movement and laid the foundation for the current Freedom Movement. Despite that fact, or perhaps because of it, elite influence is dwindling. The elite, more than anything else, is a victim of success—success that pitilessly exposed the inner contradictions of its own strategy and premises.

In the late fifties, litigation, the epitome of elite strategy, reached a point of diminishing return and it became increasingly clear that the elite had no answer to massive defiance of court orders, the spread of *de facto* segregation in the North and the widening gap between the average annual income of Negroes and whites. There may not, in fact, be any answers to these challenges within the confines of the American system. But an increasing number of Negroes are turning, in despair and in burgeoning hope, to activists who say the black elite cannot solve the problem because it is a part of the problem.

The Negro rebellion marks the coming to power of activists who are disenchanted with both the white and black power elites. It also marks a fundamental shift in Negro leadership patterns. Like all social upheavals, the Negro rebellion is not one but two revolutions—a revolution against the militant-moderate within and the reactionary without.

In the background of this shift in strategy are many elements: the root-shaking dislocations of World War II; the continuing migration to the North and West; the growth of a Negro middle class which had the foresight and ingenuity to give birth to radical children; the impact of mass media which disseminated the slogans of the "Free World"; the external pressure of a competing ideology which made an issue of humanism; and the subtle shift in America from rampant individualism to an attenuated welfare state.

These elements, and others, created the climate which made rebellion possible. But they did not create the rebellion which was a result of a parallelogram of four contextual forces:

1) The development of a new self-conception in the Negro psyche and the growth of a revolutionary will to dignity.

2) The development of a new principle of leadership which abandoned the elite concept of selected agents acting for the masses in various theaters of power.

3) The development of a social myth which provided a new script of roles and models for Negro youth.

4) The existence of a competing ideology in a

world power struggle which made wholesale repression embarrassing, if not distasteful.

To understand how these four lines of force came together, to understand how they approached each other over a period of one hundred years, we must go back a few steps and examine the dominant fact in American life—broken community.

A community is a body of people sharing common expectations and common obligations. Real community is based on reciprocity of emotion and relation between individuals sharing a common vision of the possibilities and potentialities of man. The basic fact of race relations in America is that white people and Negroes do not belong to the same community. White people, with few exceptions, do not feel that they have unqualified moral obligations to Negroes—and Negroes, in self defense, return the compliment.

The breaking of the bonds of community between Negroes and whites began in slavery and was given legal form in the Reconstruction period. In these two epochs, white power destroyed the Negro's family, annihilated his personality and consigned him to a lower order of humanity.

The seeds of the current revolution were sown in the last decade of the nineteenth century by Negro intellectuals who refused to accept the place prepared for them. In the dawn years of the twentieth century, Negro intellectuals and reform-minded whites formed an uneasy alliance. Out of this alliance came the National Association for the Advancement of Colored People and the National Urban League.

The old protest movement, as distinguished from

the new Freedom Movement, was an invention of the militants and moderates of the League and the NAACP. Of crucial importance in the context of the postslavery Negro renaissance was the work of the NAACP. By organizing a bold legal campaign, the NAACP opened the eyes of Negroes to a whole new vista of struggle. But the NAACP and the Urban League were organized around a narrow principle of leadership. Both organizations were composed largely of middle- and upper-income Negroes and whites who were somewhat removed from the masses. And it was from the masses that the first revolutionary impulse came.

During the first two decades of the twentieth century, Negroes were groping in some dim, obscure way toward an understanding of their role in American life. A feeling was growing in the backwoods of the South—a feeling that life could be better, brighter and more meaningful. The mood crystallized in 1915-16 in a mass migration which has continued to this day. The great Negro Migration—the most significant population upheaval since the wagon trains rolled West—changed the shape of race relations. It nationalized the race problem, gave the Negro a base of political power in the North and set the stage for our present confrontation.

World War I, following close on the heels of the black migrants, shattered the old racial equilibrium. After that war, it was no longer possible for Negroes to avoid the issue of their place in American life. The treatment of Negro soldiers in Europe and the hostile environment to which they returned made a permanent impress on the Negro mind. So did the Red Summer of 1919, a summer of terror and blood and twenty-six race riots.

If World War I was not the beginning of Negro emancipation, it was, at least, the beginning of wisdom. The war abroad and the quiet war at home gave birth to the New Negro Revolt of the twenties which was a little miniature of the revolt of the sixties. There were three identical phases: a literary revival that focused attention on the Negro folk tradition, a student revolt that began at Fisk and spread to other colleges and a black nationalist crusade which was America's first Negro mass movement.

The lightning of the Great Depression, following the thunderclap of World War I, illuminated the precarious ledge on which the Negro existed. In the light of this event, Negroes looked at themselves and knew themselves—and they were naked. Aside from dreary statistics and sociological jargon that hides more than it reveals, the psychological fact was shattering. And it hovers somewhere in the deeps of the Negro psyche.

The first fruit of despair was a shift in strategy. The elite methods of litigation and lobbying were repudiated. Hungry youth took to the streets, picketing, boycotting and demonstrating. A harbinger of things to come, and a revelation of the depth of Negro despair, was the Harlem riot of 1935 in which Negroes blindly smashed glass—and can it be doubted?—idols.

World War II accelerated the fury. At the very beginning of that conflict, Negroes made it clear that they were tired of making the world safe for a commodity that was in short supply at home. The period between 1940 and 1943 was remarkably similar to the period between 1960 and 1963. Mass meetings were held, stores were picketed and spirituals were sung. A. Philip Randolph, the spiritual father of the current movement, electrified America with a call for a nonviolent civil disobedience movement. Randolph's call struck a responsive chord in the hearts of young Americans who were tired of petitioning and resolving. Several organizations were founded in these years to agitate for a new departure. The most significant was the Congress of Racial Equality (CORE) which staged its first sit-in in Chicago in 1942. The whole pageant of accelerated defiance reached a pitch in 1947 with a NAACP appeal to the United Nations. The audacity of activists in 1948-49 (the Peekskill riots, the Progressive party and A. Philip Randolph's call for a civil disobedience movement against the draft) caused widespread concern. The Civil Rights Report of 1947, the Democratic party plank of 1948 and the integration of the armed forces were, in part, attempts to contain Negro discontent which was taking a dangerous and unpredictable turn.

Although it apparently failed, the revolt of the forties was, in effect, a huge dress rehearsal for the upheaval that came a decade later. The experiences of the forties roused the Negro masses from their lethargy and taught them lessons they would never forget.

The thirties and the forties: these were the truly decisive years in the Negro odyssey. The epoch from 1930 to 1945 shook the Negro ghetto to its foundation, giving rise to estrangement, alienation and thought. The Negro emerged in this period as a questing social being with an awareness of his strength and his situation. Everything in Negro life marked the change—the publication of *Native Son,* the radical alteration in the texture of modern jazz, the militant posture of Negro youth and the mushroom growth of nationalist movements.

All these changes occurred between 1930 and 1945. In that fifteen-year period, there was a greater change in the Negro psyche than in the whole period between 1860 and 1930. By the end of the forties, it was apparent to almost everyone that the Negro had moved within himself. Myrdal put his finger on the inner emigration early in the war. Said he: "America can never more regard its Negroes as a patient, submissive minority. Negroes will continually become less well accommodated. They will organize for defense and offense. They will be more vociferous. They will watch their opportunities ever more keenly."

The new mood in the ghetto was a function of many variables, some external and some internal. In the great world beyond the Atlantic and the Pacific, there was a shrinkage of the white ego which reached the limits of its four-hundred-year expansion. There was, contrariwise, an expansion of the Negro ghetto at home, an expansion expressed most vividly in the lava-like march of Negro ghettos to the city limits of a hundred municipalities.

These two movements, external contraction and internal distension, changed race relations forever.

Negroes and whites began to look at each other in different ways. And they began, each in his own way, to prepare for the confrontation to come.

There was, in sum, a radical new conception at work in the ghetto, a conception that reflected an equally radical alteration in the Negro mood. The Big Change in Negro life occurred not in the sixties but in the forties. The only things wanting were a voice to give tongue to it, an instrument to contain it and a detonating spark. The detonating spark was the Supreme Court decision of 1954 which was the result of a long and brilliant legal campaign by the NAACP. This decision reopened the national compromise of 1877 and essayed a new definition of the Negro's status in American life. It was followed the next year by the Montgomery bus boycott, out of which came a new ideology and a remarkable fisher of men, Martin Luther King, Jr.

Montgomery was a great myth, in the best sense of the word. It was a womb from which emerged a corpus of models and images to which growth could aspire.

Montgomery and the Supreme Court decisions were key elements in the growth cycle of a new generation, a generation, it should be noted, that had never known the white man when he was not hard pressed, a generation born and raised in the fateful break between two epochs.

This generation came to seed in an era of bad faith. It became apparent soon after 1954 that the Supreme Court decision was not going to be obeyed. There began the whole dreary ritual of September sickness, of skirmishes in schoolyards, of troops and tanks and despair. A certain hope died in these years. A certain faith. There was a convulsion of the collective mind.

To make matters worse, the economic situation became menacing. With the beginning of a series of "economic downturns," the Negro was pushed back toward the well-remembered days of the thirties. More ominous was the day-to-day aggression of automation.

Another milestone on the road to Birmingham, a cause and an effect of the mood of despair and desperation, was the rise of the Black Muslims. Not many Negroes were impressed by the Muslims' call for total separation. But almost all Negroes were touched by their savage indictment of hypocrisy and their delicious acceptance of the fact of being black.

In this climate, four young men sat down in Greensboro, North Carolina, and a whole generation began the long and painful process of standing up. The sit-in movement raced across the South, scoring unheard-of successes. More importantly, three organizations—the Student Nonviolent Coordinating Committee (SNICK), the Congress of Racial Equality and the Southern Christian Leadership Conference—came forward to give tone and direction to the agony and the fervor of the most significant youth movement in American history.

In 1960-61, the rivulets of hope and ambition began to descend from their secret places in the high mountains of Negro despair. Then it was that myth, self-conception, leadership, and external pressure mated.

From Martin Luther King, Jr., came the non-violent ideology (based not so much on Gandhi as the Baptist church) and the idea that every man was responsible for his own freedom and that he could not discharge that responsibility by contributing two dollars to an organization and voting on resolutions once a year. SNICK contributed the concept of the professional rebel, of the man or woman or child who abandoned place, position and prestige to fight on the front lines for a subsistence wage. From SNICK also came the concept of "going to the people" and living with them in order to organize and create indigenous leadership. CORE brought a long history of direct action to the marriage and a tough-talking, tough-acting stance.

The struggle moved now from courtrooms to the streets, from litigation to demonstrations. One phase followed another: the sit-ins leading to the Freedom Rides and the Freedom Rides leading to Albany, Georgia, which led to Birmingham and confrontation.

The movement grew on what it fed on, escalating goals and making them seem higher. The more the activists gained, the more they wanted. The more they protested, the more they wanted to protest. The more they won, the more they wanted to win.

Negroes of all ranks were swept along by the dancing waves of discontent. Like a sensitizing symbol, like a grandiose myth, the Freedom Movement set up a lively exchange of influences, the first effect of which was to create a mood, a *Stimmung*, a collective state of mind, to which each individual contributed and by which each was moulded.

In the crucible of collective excitement, the bony structure of Negro belief and habit became soft and was pushed into new and more aggressive shapes. Under the impact of the mood, Negroes became more suggestible, more malleable and more responsive to new stimulation and new ideas. Their circle of claims on society widened and a new racial self arose to supplement and include individual racial selves. Movement and mood sustained and reinforced each other, creating new roles and self-conceptions by which individual Negroes could measure themselves.

To the immense influence of the new mood must be added the factor of success. As the movement moved from success to success, there was a progressive widening of the circle of combatants and an increasing audacity of vision.

Propelled by these psychic dynamisms, the movement leaped in 1963-1964 from crisis to crisis, escalating the racial problems to new frontiers of strife and controversy.

The leaping waves of discontent and direct action pose large problems of analysis. Is the Freedom Movement, for example, a revolution?

There can be no neat and categorical answer to this question. Every revolution creates its own path and demands judgment on its own terms. This is particularly true of a nonviolent revolution on the part of an oppressed minority which does not intend to take over a government but to fulfill it—a distinction, to be sure, that gives small comfort to defenders of the status quo. For the black rebels are demanding not a token but a complete change in things as they are.

A revolution, in essence, is a rapid but not necessarily violent social change through which the power relations of social groups are changed and a new order established. The main criterion of a revolution is a desire and a will on the part of a group to force a fundamental change in the social order.

Judged by these standards, the Freedom Movement assumes a different face. Almost all active members of the movement desire a basic change in the social order. Not all, however, have a revolutionary will. Whether this will crystallizes or not depends to a great extent on our responses. For the main goal of the movement is a basic change in the power relations between Negro and white Americans.

It is not noted often enough that power relations between Negroes and whites have already changed. The Negro today is the dominant social fact in almost every metropolitan community of any size. He elects scores of mayors from Nashville and Atlanta to Chicago and Detroit; he provides the margin of profit for thousands of businesses; and his voice is often decisive in American Presidential elections.

These are surface manifestations of a basic shift in the real position of American Negroes. The Negro upheaval, like most revolutions, is an attempt to force recognition of a change which has already occurred, a change which is stymied by obsolescent social arrangements and outmoded institutions.

The Freedom Movement has already forced a minor realignment in Negro-white power relations. Since the beginning of the sit-in age, there has been a shift in the relations between Negro and white Americans. More concessions have been made to *Negro power* since 1960 than in any comparable period in the history of America.

The 1960-64 convulsion, to sum up, meets some of the basic tests of a classic upheaval: the direct intervention of the masses, for example, and the reliance on direct action which is, to the Freedom Movement, what Clausewitz called war: a continuation of politics by other means.

Tactics, strategy, objectives: all point to a petit revolution straining on the edge of an open confrontation. But the movement, so far, has not solved the two basic problems that would make it a real revolution: the organization of a sustained national resistance movement and the mobilization of the so-called underclass in the great concrete ghettos. For this reason and others, primarily the limitations of the Negro situation, it would be more accurate to call the upheaval a rebellion, a turning away from, a going out of—a becoming.

Semantics apart, the cataclysm in the streets is real enough, and it proceeds from revolutionary premises. The fundamental premise is that old forms and old ways are no longer adequate and that the social system, as organized, is incapable of solving, through normal channels, the urgent problem presented to it by history. The second major premise is allied to the first: that the social system, as organized, is part of the problem and cannot be appealed to or relied upon as an independent arbiter in power conflicts of which it is a part. The third major premise is that white Americans, generally speaking, lack the will, the courage, and the intelligence to voluntarily grant Negroes their civil rights and that they must be forced to do it by pressure.

Here are the minor premises:

1) That people do not discriminate for the fun of it, that the function of prejudice is to defend interests (social, economic, political and psychological interests) and that appeals to the fair play of prejudiced people are prayers said to the wind.

2) That communities will change discriminatory patterns if they are forced to make a clear-cut choice between bias and another highly cherished value—economic gain, education or civic peace.

3) That struggle and conflict are necessary for social change, that showdown situations are desirable because they throw the whole range of race relations into the arena of public discussion.

4) That the constitutional rights of live human beings are at stake and that these rights are neither ballotable nor negotiable; that negotiation, to be meaningful, must take place between equals acting in good faith and that the issues here are precisely equality and the good faith, if not the good sense, of white Americans.

5) That peace is the presence of community and not the absence of conflict; and that demonstrations against Jim Crow are attempts to establish peace and not breaches of the peace which, according to black rebels, has never existed anywhere and at anytime between black and white Americans.

We may or may not agree with these premises. It doesn't matter, really. For what we must realize now is that the burden of proof is on us. The face of the Commonwealth gives abundant testimony of the total failure of the politics of good intentions. What we must do now is to examine our own inarticulate premises and our own involvement or lack of involvement in a struggle that goes to the heart of our meaning as a people.

We stand now in a lull in the lurch of history. The barometer drops so low before a storm. No man wants a storm, but wishing will not sweep away the clouds. If we do not act, the storm will come— if not now, five years from now; if not then, ten years later. There has been, as we have seen, a Negro revolt in every decade of this century. Each revolt failed, only to emerge in the next decade on a higher level of development. It is not to our best interest for the current rebellion to fail. For one hesitates to speculate on the form and intensity a Negro revolt will take in the seventies and eighties when Negroes form a majority in many of our major cities.

We are heading now for a land no American has traversed. For perhaps the first time in our history, we have a thoroughly restive minority population on our hands. So far we have done our best to bring out the worst in urban Negroes who are strategically placed to cause social chaos. Negroes, for the most part, inhabit the inner cores of America's largest cities; and they hold the key to the future of the city and the future of American democracy. If we do not want a black Ireland here, if we do not want our cities divided into mutually hostile casbahs, if we do not want the Negro rebellion to become a real revolution, then we must dare to flesh out the words we profess.

This is an important moment in the history of the Commonwealth. There stretch out before us two roads and two roads only. America must now become America or something else, a Fourth Reich perhaps, or a Fourth Reich of the spirit. To put the matter bluntly, we must become what we say we are or give in to the secret dream that blights our hearts.

Let us not deceive ourselves. The problem before us now is not the Negro but ourselves; not civil rights but the city; not love but the creation of that America which could have been and should have been and never was.

II

STRUCTURE:

The Black Establishment

RACE RELATIONS in America are relations between ruling elites.

Issues are resolved, boundaries are marked off, favors are granted and pleas are denied by men of substance and power on both sides of the racial line.

Negroes and whites in America, Gunnar Myrdal observed, deal with each other, like two foreign countries, "through the medium of plenipotentiaries." What is also true, and more to the point, is that Negroes and whites deal with each other through the medium of competing power structures.

Like two foreign countries, like hostile and suspicious strangers, Negroes and whites negotiate treaties and truces through separate but not quite equal power blocs. The white power structure has been endlessly annotated and analyzed. But little or no attention has been given to the Negro power structure as a group of self-conscious moulders and shapers of racial policy.

The importance of the Negro power structure can hardly be overemphasized. It is, in fact, a parallel government which fills the vacuum that exists between Negro citizens and the state. Plenipotentiaries of this shadow government—which we shall call the Black Establishment—have negotiated with the League of Nations and addressed formal notes to the United Nations. During World War II, the NAACP—the offensive arm of the Establishment—negotiated with the government of England and addressed formal letters to Sir Winston Churchill.

In times of crisis—and it has always been a time of crisis for the Negro—black men ask not what their country can do for them but what the Black Establishment can do for them.

The Black Establishment, oddly enough, is not all-black. It is a group of Negroes *and whites* who command the power lines *in* the Negro community: the executive secretaries, the board chairmen (often white), the presidents (often white), and board members (Negro and white) of protest and improvement associations; the bishops of Negro denominations and the pastors of the largest and most influential churches (the two are not necessarily synonymous) the editors and publishers of major Negro newspapers and periodicals; the leading educators, business and professional men.

The key members of this group from the standpoint of racial policy are the executive officers and board of directors of the protest and improvement association and the leading editors and publishers. It helps enormously if a new departure in the Negro community is sanctioned by these structures of power. On the other hand, it is difficult, though not impossible, to carry new ground if the Black Establishment says no.

Although the power and influence of the Establishment ranges over the whole theater of Negro life, the focal points are concentrated in five cities. Washington, Atlanta, and Nashville are important as centers of ideas, programs and recruits. New York and Chicago, on the other hand, are control centers. The importance of being a New Yorker is dramatized by the board of one protest organization. Eighteen of the twenty-three national board members come from New York City and environs.

What are the prerequisites for membership in the group?

Money helps, but many moneyed men are not members, and many members are not moneyed men. As in the white world, control of a major institution —a protest group, a major business or a church— is extremely important.

For our purposes then, an Establishment member (and we are concerned here only with the national Establishment) is a person who holds a key office (president, executive vice president, secretary, treasurer, board chairman or board membership) in a major educational, business, defense or improvement association.

These men and women are the decision makers for the Negro community. But there are men who decide for the decision makers, elites, in other words, within the elite. A member of the inner core of power holds an independent base of power and membership on the governing boards of one or more key national institutions.

How does one recognize an Establishment man?

By the boards he acquires. Here is a power pro-

file of Channing Heggie Tobias, one of the least
known and most powerful Negroes in recent history.
Note particularly the signs of Establishment grace:
membership on governing boards.

Channing H. Tobias (1882-1961), social worker,
educator, national decision maker. Student secretary,
International Commission of YWCA, 1911-23; Senior
secretary for colored work of YMCA of USA, 1923-46;
director, Phelps-Stokes Fund, 1946-52; Member,
President Truman's Civil Rights Committee, 1946-
47; Alternate delegate, United Nations, 1951-52;
Member, governing boards (board of directors or
board of trustees) of following organizations and
institutions: NAACP (chairman), Marshall Field
Foundation, Jessie Smith Noyes Foundation, Liberia
Company, Hampton Institute, Howard University,
Paine College, Palmer Memorial Institute, Na-
tional Council of Churches of Christ in USA, and the
Commercial State Bank and Trust Company of New
York.

The important thing to note in this power pro-
file is what sociologists call "the accumulation of
advantages," an unnecessarily obscure phrase for
the admirably simple biblical rule: "To them that
hath, more will be given." What this means in terms
of national Negro power is that influence in one
sphere can be transferred to influence in another
sphere. Prominent educators and bishops, for example, often serve on the boards of directors of
major business and protest and defense organizations. And powerful businessmen, in turn, often
serve on the boards of trustees of educational
and philanthropic organizations.

Contrary to the generally accepted opinion, power does not inhere in individuals. Without access to institutionalized power, individuals are powerless in both the Negro and white community. The popular error is to confuse prominence or wealth with power. These things, as we have shown, are convertible into power over racial policy. But they are not in themselves instrumentalities of national power. Some politicians, for example, hold local power. But they are not usually members of the national Establishment. Nor are politicians, as politicians (Adam Powell, Jr., excepted), fertile in raising and disposing of large issues bearing on national racial policy.

One makes a great leap into an understanding of the Establishment if one perceives why Adam Clayton Powell, Sr. was admitted to the Establishment while his son, Adam, with greater fame and greater local power, was excluded. Powell the elder sat for many, many years on Establishment boards; the son has not yet occupied a seat in the inner sanctum. Relevant here are questions of style and temperament as well as availability. Powell has, over the years, complained bitterly of Establishment "snubs." And he has discovered repeatedly that Establishment games are played by Establishment rules.

What precisely are Establishment rules?

Why, for example, are a Richmond doctor and a New York City judge more influential in shaping national racial policy than, say, Congressman William L. Dawson or Congressman Adam Clayton Powell, Jr.?

The core answer is that the doctor and the judge are members of the little-known inner core of Establishment power. Both are among the ten men and one woman who were on the NAACP board in 1943 and who were still listed twenty years later in 1963. More importantly, both men were members of the executive committee of the board in 1963. The New York judge, though little known nationally, has ranged over the whole arena of Establishment power. He was a founder and incorporator of the NAACP Legal Defense and Educational Fund and he is a former member of the executive committee of the Urban League board.

Through the doctor and the judge we come to the heart of the matter: continuous service in Establishment circles. Board members in every organization come and go. The names that turn up year after year are important: they indicate centers of power and influence. More importantly, they point to the hierarchies within the hierarchy.

The governing boards of Establishment organizations change periodically, but the surface changes hide a steel core of continuity. There is, as Professor N. P. Tillman, Jr., pointed out in a study of the NAACP, an inner core of men who hold board seats for years and then, dying, hand over the torch to another core. In a study of the 186 persons elected to the board through 1954, Professor Tillman focused on "the nuclei of active minorities which dominated the Board in the two periods, 1910-29 and 1929-55." He concluded: "Between 1910 and 1929, the nucleus appears to have consisted of: John Milholland (d., 1922), Walter Sachs (1912-15),

Joel Spingarn, Arthur Spingarn, William E. Walling,
John H. Holmes, Mary Ovington, Oswald Villard,
and W. E. B. Du Bois. . . . All but the first carried
over into the second period, both as Board members
and general officers, thus providing continuity of
personnel and policy. In the second period they
were joined by others, predominantly Negro (5-2),
namely: Louis Wright, Charles Toney, Allan Chalmers, Alfred Lewis, Channing Tobias, Theodore
Spaulding, and perhaps Robert Weaver. Meanwhile,
some of the holdovers died or resigned among whom
only Du Bois was forced out (in 1934) for 'the good
of the Association.' "

What emerges from all this is the power of Establishment boards and the relative weakness of
men, whatever their local power or influence, who
do not participate in the informal give-and-take
that precedes decision and the formal voting that
ratifies it. The only exceptions to this are major publishers who can make their weight felt without
formal entree into board rooms. Oftentimes, in fact,
radical departures in Negro policy are cleared in
advance with key publishers. Before a white ad-
ministrator was named to head an Establishment
agency, the appointment was cleared by long-distance calls to a handful of men across the country.
But this exception proves the rule. The men who
received long-distance calls were not asked to vote
on the appointment (the board had already voted);
they were asked to close ranks behind an Establishment *fait accompli*.

We return then to the major premise. Men remote
from the board rooms do not vote; and men who

do not vote in the small groups where one vote makes a difference do not generally count. This is not to say that national boards are the final arbiters of racial policy. The ruling boards of the Establishment are free to decide policy within certain limits prescribed by other institutions within the family of power in the Negro world. Of vast importance in this connection are Negro educational institutions. Negro educators have always exerted tremendous influence on racial policy. The nature of this influence was dramatized by the sit-ins which led to the expulsion of hundreds of students and the firing of scores of teachers.

The family of power includes not only Negro organizations but white organizations. Racial policy is subtly shaped and diluted by the expectations, priorities and fears of liberal, labor, religious, and minority groups. From this white liberal nexus, the Establishment seeks allies and donations. The most talented of these allies have definite ideas about the goals and direction of Negro policy. And it is not always possible to accept the donations without accepting the donor's program.

Among the leading organizations in this shadow cabinet of the shadow cabinet are the UAW and other liberal unions, the American Civil Liberties Union, the American Jewish Committee and the American Jewish Congress, the race relations departments (under various names) of the YWCA, YMCA, the National Council of Churches, the Roman Catholic Church and the American Friends Service Committee.

Another layer of hidden power on the fringes of

the Establishment centers in philanthropic organizations and their representatives. The Rosenwald Foundation, the American Missionary Association of the Congregationalist Church, the Rockefeller foundations and the Harmon Fund have played huge roles in shaping and braking Negro policy. Of crucial importance in the context of current power realities are the Taconic Foundation and the Phelps-Stokes Fund.

These organizations and their representatives are part of the formal and informal network of power surrounding the core organizations of the Establishment. Some of these groups send white delegates to the Establishment. Some groom specially selected Negroes *who represent them* in the inner councils of power.

White delegates to the Establishment should not be confused with bona fide members of the Establishment. Certain positions in the Establishment are apparently reserved for white men. The NAACP, the National Urban League and the NAACP Legal Defense Fund have never had a Negro president or a Negro treasurer. Nor for that matter have many other Negro institutions of power. Final control (chairman of the board) and financial control (treasurer and chairman of the financial and investment committees) of Negro colleges are generally vested in white hands. One Eastern investment banker, for instance, is chairman of the board of one Negro college, president and treasurer of the board of another and a member of the investment and executive committee of a third. Although this trustee holds enormous power in the Negro world, his name seldom, if ever, appears in a Negro newspaper.

Analysis of white power in the black world is complicated by primogenital relationships. No Negro family, for example, has exerted greater influence on Negro policy than the Baldwins, the Rosenwalds or the Spingarns.

William H. Baldwin the elder was a close and influential advisor of Booker T. Washington. His wife, Ruth Standish Baldwin, was a founder of the National Urban League. Lester Granger said she did more than any other person to shape the basic philosophy of the Urban League. Since that time, there has always been a Baldwin on the Urban League board.

The Spingarns have made a great contribution to Negro welfare and they have held power positions commensurate with their contributions. Dr. Joel E. Spingarn, an erudite professor of English, served as treasurer and chairman of the board of the NAACP before assuming the presidency which he held from 1929 to his death in 1939. He was succeeded as president by his brother, Arthur (1878-   ), and as a board member by his widow, Amy.

The Spingarns are to the NAACP what the Baldwins are to the Urban League. In other words, there has always been a Spingarn on the NAACP board. In fact, for almost fifty years, there have been two Spingarns on the NAACP board. Arthur Spingarn, the current NAACP president, was chairman of the legal committee for more than twenty years. He was also a founder, incorporator and first president of the NAACP Legal Defense Fund.

Other white men in black power in the years of the rebellion were:

Allan Knight Chalmers (1897-), New York City, professor, Congregational minister, author. President of the NAACP Legal Defense Fund; former head of the Scottsboro Defense Committee, former co-chairman of the National Council for a Permanent FEPC; one time member of more than thirty governing boards.

Jack Greenberg (1925-), New York City, attorney. Executive director of NAACP Legal Defense Fund; former associate director of the Fund.

Henry Steeger (1903-), New York City, publisher of *Argosy* magazine. President of National Urban League (1961-64).

Lindsley S. Kimball (1894-), New York City foundation executive succeeded Steeger as National Urban League President, August, 1964.

Stephen Currier (1931-), New York City, philanthropist. President of Taconic Foundation; co-chairman of Council for United Civil Rights Leadership. Organizer of fund-raising project for major civil rights organizations.

Other influential and well-heeled whites (poor whites, like poor Negroes, are democratically excluded) shape Negro policy and exercise veto power on new issues through their positions as board members and patrons and links to the white power structure.

The counterparts of the white friends in power are Roy Wilkins (1901-), an ex-newspaper editor who is executive secretary of the NAACP; Whitney Young, Jr. (1921-), a former social worker and educator who is executive director of the National Urban League and co-chairman of the Council for United Civil Rights Leadership. Also influential on the national scene, though not in the limelight, are:

Frederick Douglass Patterson (1901-), New York City, veterinarian, educator, foundation executive. President of Phelps-Stokes Fund; president of National Business League; president-emeritus of Tuskegee Institute; founder and former president of the United Negro College Fund; board of trustees, Bennett College, Bethune-Cookman College, Hampton Institute, Palmer Memorial, Southern Educational Foundation.

Ralph Johnson Bunche (1904-), New York City, political scientist, UN official. Board of directors, NAACP; Phelps-Stokes Fund; Board of Higher Education, New York; Fund for Advancement of Education; Rockefeller Foundation; Harvard University Board of Overseers.

Stephen Gill Spottswood (1896-), Washington, D.C., AME Zion bishop. Chairman of board of directors of NAACP.

Ralph J. Bunche, among others, has sharply criticized the role of white men in Negro affairs. In a 1940 memorandum prepared for the Myrdal study, Bunche said white men exercised a great deal of control over the selection of Negro leaders and scholars. He went on to criticize the whole philosophy of interracial liberalism. White members of interracial organizations, he wrote, usually "fix the measure of value" of the organization, deciding not merely the question of how much to ask for "but also how to ask and, indeed, whether the Negro should ask at all."

Similar attacks have come from Carter Woodson, W. E. B. Du Bois, E. Franklin Frazier and others. All echoed, in varying degrees, the charge of Jessie O. Thomas who said once that interracial cooperation often ends up with Negroes coo-ing and white people operating.

Bunche, in particular, was scathing (in the 1940 memorandum) in his criticism of interracial liberalism. Too often, Bunche said, in a criticism often repeated in the sixties, Negro board members receive their cues from white board members. In general, he concluded, concern for the opinion of white supporters and allies is a powerful factor in keeping Negro organizations respectable.

Establishment arbiters denied these criticisms in the forties and they deny them today. In their support, it should be said that some whites in the Establishment are more militant than some Negroes. Jack Greenberg, for example, is one of the more militant members of the legal wing; and Herbert Hill is perhaps the most radical member of the national staff of the NAACP. Other examples could be cited: a former National Urban League board member who championed a more militant Urban League policy at a time when some, though not all, Negro board members were opposed.

And yet, when all this is said, the fact remains that most white members of the Establishment are moderate. Whites, as a group, have served as a brake rather than as an accelerator of the Freedom Movement.

It would be a mistake, however, to blame white liberals and moderates for Establishment style. The Establishment, in its present form, is an invention of two radically different men, Booker T. Washington and W. E. B. Du Bois, and it betrays the tensions of this extraordinary miscegenation between conservatism and militancy. In the first decades of the twentieth century, Booker T. Washington established an entente between "moderate" Negroes and "the better element of whites." In this same period, Du Bois established a similar entente between "militant" Negroes and "liberal" whites. After Washington's death, these divergent forces met at Joel Spingarn's country home in Dutchess County, New York, and decided, in so many words, that Booker T. Washington and W. E. B. Du Bois were both right and that all roads leading to the goal were equally honorable. This, of course, was no decision at all and Du Bois, perceiving this eighteen years later, left the Establishment with a blast at the ruling group.

The basic problem in *L'affaire* Du Bois was not program but style. To understand Establishment style we must hold two contradictory ideas at the center of our minds. The Establishment is both militant and conservative. Its pronouncements, in other words, are militant; but its actions are cautious and conciliatory.

What distinguishes the Negro power structure, above all, is its reluctance to act. This powerful group, whose tentacles extend into every area of Negro life, rarely raises new issues (FEPC, nonviolence, sit-ins, mass demonstrations, don't-buy-where-you-can't-work came from without). Through the years, the dominant voices in the Negro power structure have been voices of caution and compromise. Through the years, the manipulators of the structure have been men too timid and too cautious to initiate and direct action.

The Establishment's word, *protest,* is a mask for inaction. The deepest strain in Establishment protest is sterile and socially irrelevant. Endless debate, polite petitions, the sending of telegrams and letters, the whole ritual of mimeograph machines and type-writers: all this has been a substitute for hard analysis and risky action. The word *risk:* this separates the Establishment and its perennial critics, activists. The Establishment has never been willing to take serious risks. It has never been willing to jeopardize place, position and institutions in adventures for freedom. As a result, there has hovered over all Establishment activities a faint smell of gamesmanship, of pretense and posturing and evasions of reality. It was this, I think, that led Myrdal and Bunche to write two of the most mournful sentences in the whole history of leadership description and analysis.

1) Bunche: ". . . leadership itself is a form of escape."

2) Myrdal: "The Negro hates the Negro role in American society, and the Negro leader, who acts out this role in public life, becomes the symbol of what the Negro hates."

There are endless stories on the game aspect of Establishment leadership. The best one, I think, used to bring down the house on the old vaudeville circuit. A Negro comedian, mimicking "a big Negro leader," would begin the following sentence in a stentorian voice and gradually lower his voice until at the end it was a bare whisper:

"What we colored FOLKS have got to do is to RISE UP AND STRIKE DOWN these here damned white folks."

Since the establishment of the Establishment, Negro leadership has been under constant attack. No serious student of the Negro ethos has failed to note what Drake and Cayton called "the ritual condemnation of Negro leadership." Day in and day out, from barber shop, bar and beauty shop, the cry arises: Negro leadership—the people who run things, i. e., the Negro Establishment—is no good.

A great deal of this constant and sometimes petty criticism stems from the social distance between the leadership and the masses. Students of power say that a people always get the kind of leadership they deserve. But the reverse is also true: leaders, in the long run, get the kind of followers they deserve.

The main bone of contention between the Establishment and its critics revolves around the cumbersome word—masses. Garvey (in the twenties), Bunche (in the forties), A. Philip Randolph (in the forties), E. Franklin Frazier (in the fifties), and rebellious students (in the sixties) have contended that the Establishment is a conspiracy in contempt of the masses. However that may be, it is certain that the Establishment has never solved what Du Bois called gingerly "the inner problem of contact with their own lower classes." Bunche went further and said (in the forties), that the Negro elite "knows little, if any, more about the Negro in the mass than does the average white man."

The question at issue, however, is not knowledge but use. The Establishment has never organized the masses for social contention. Down through the years, the Negro power structure has been more active in accommodating the masses to misery than in organizing them for an attack on the forces responsible for the misery. The riots of 1964 illuminated the deep chasm between Negro men of power and the Negro masses.

Establishment statements point to a deep fear of direct intervention on the part of the masses. The fear is not altogether unreasonable, and it is not a fear of the Establishment alone. Some of the new organizations, trembling on the verge of risky action, have shrunk back shuddering from the abyss into which they had just peered.

Behind all the words and all the slogans is a terrible reality: millions on millions of men and women with deep fears and resentments and needs —fears and resentments and needs, it should be noted, that cannot be met by the appointment of a Negro federal judge or the filing of a court suit. No one knows really what will happen if this force is loosed. For members of the lowest stratum of the Negro working class do not belong to any organization. Not even, despite current propaganda, the church.

How bitter are these men and women?

How far are they willing to go?

If they are set in motion, can they be controlled?

Many men, not all of them members of the Establishment, have asked themselves these questions and have decided, in good conscience, that they would rather not know the answers.

The Establishment says officially that the Negro masses cannot be organized, that they are utterly apathetic and demoralized. What this means, unofficially, is that it is impossible to organize the masses around a "responsible," "respectable," "moderate" program—around the Establishment's program, in short. In essence, the Establishment's program is a program of agency relation, of carefully selected agents acting for the masses in the courts and other theaters of power. The central weakness of this program—and Establishment men are too brilliant not to know it—is that men cannot be freed by agents—white or black.

The ever-recurring cry of the Negro power structure, and some of the new organizations have taken it up, is "Deal with us or the radicals will take over." This is a curious confession of programmatic and ideological poverty. The statement, as a statement of leadership, tells much about the relationships between the masses and the men who claim to be their leaders.

Over the years, Negro men of power have built up considerable good will with the white power structure. They have access to the state house and the White House and the sources of white money. And this access enables them to get small favors for the people they say they are leading.

Activists, surprisingly enough, admit the existence of this good will. But they contend that power and prestige are capital and, like capital, must be invested and risked occasionally if it is to bring a proper return.

At issue here are deep questions of power ethics. Power works the same way everywhere and men respond to power in the same way everywhere. "Outs," for example, tend to be radical; "ins" tend to be conservative. The same rule applies to organizations. Experience suggests that reform organizations cannot stand too much success. The more a reform organization wins, the more money it collects, the more staffers it acquires, the more conservative it generally becomes.

Establishment ("in") style can best be understood in a comparison with activist ("out") style. Activists seek a *showdown;* the Establishment seeks an *accommodation.* The Establishment says it is necessary to *reduce* racial tensions; activists say it is necessary to *raise them* to the highest pitch.

Activists *denounce* white people; the Establishment *appeals* to their sense of fair play. Activists call for a *revolt;* the Establishment calls for a *conference.* Activists appeal to the *masses;* the Establishment appeals to *"the better people."* Activists *march;* the Establishment *confers;* Activists *demonstrate;* The Establishment *negotiates.* Activists *demand;* the Establishment *resolves.* Activists are *radical* (In the Latin sense of root); the Establishment is *conservative*—militantly so.

Although the Establishment resists new ideas, it contains many bold—and some radical—men. To say that the group is moribund and reactionary is to simplify a complicated process. Reactionaries have always been members of the Establishment, but so have progressives. Atlanta Life Insurance Company, for example, sponsored many forward-looking developments in Atlanta. Supreme Life financed and carried to the Supreme Court, through Earl B. Dickerson, a key restrictive covenant case.

Prominent members of the inner core have supported non-E causes and some, like Dickerson, Thurgood Marshall, Ralph Bunche, W. H. Hastie, and John H. Johnson, have made laudable efforts to move the structure in the direction of the dominant social challenge, the Negro masses. Men who see a simple black-white dichotomy between the Establishment and radicals would do well to ponder the actions of E-men during World War II. Dickerson and Hastie resigned important government positions as protest against discrimination; "radical" representatives of labor protested, but did not resign.

Other independent Establishment men include two powerful editors who continued to print news about Paul Robeson in the fifties. Equally independent was an insurance executive who disavowed *the ideas* of the elder Du Bois but refused to disavow the man—at a time when many "radicals" were running for cover.

But here, as elsewhere, rank has its privileges.

And here, as elsewhere, the exceptions prove the rule.

What matters in the Establishment is not the individual but the group. As a structure of power, as a self-conscious determiner of Negro policy, the Establishment moves slowly, views all new ideas and departures with suspicion, if not hostility.

Like men of power everywhere, Establishmentarians are victims of their fears and phobias. They would rather see things not happen than to see them happen. They are, in short, Hamlets who "prefer to bear those ills they have than to fly to others they know not of." And yet, like Hamlet, they can be goaded into action.

One of the most important decisions in the history of American Negroes, the mid-forties decision to attack segregation per se in the courts, was made by a handful of E-men in a Manhattan hotel room. Among the decision makers were the late Walter White, Thurgood Marshall and W. H. Hastie.

The decision made by these men and others was later ratified by a larger group. That the Establishment was able to initiate and carry this radical new departure (until then the dominant issue in Negro life was separate-but-equal facilities) despite strong opposition from men in local power structures indicates the power and the potential of the group.

Although members sometimes meet behind closed doors and make large decisions affecting the lives and livelihoods of the Negro masses, the Establishment is not a conspiracy. Most decisions, in fact, are unconscious extensions of Establishment style, decisions that crystallize and take shape without a vote or, indeed, an articulated proposal.

Members of the Establishment are, by and large, men who look out on life from the same vantage point. As managers of men and/or material and as holders of real estate and stocks and bonds, Establishment men are moulded by the same forces and respond to events with the same style. Like their contemporaries in the white world, like men of place and power and property everywhere, they tend to fear men and issues that rock the boat.

Establishment policy is not entirely a matter of common temperament. Since the Armenia Conference of 1916—a Negro unity conference called by a white man, Joel Spingarn—the Negro power structure has been a self-conscious group composed of men of weight who make decisions with other men of weight in mind. And more: men in the inner circle know each other, see each other socially, play bridge and poker together and decide affairs of state and money over martinis and Scotch. When the late President Kennedy invited Negro leaders to the White House for the Emancipation centennial celebration, Negro guests—from North, South, East and West—greeted each other with the warmth of long-lost cousins as, indeed, many of them were. An administrative official, dimly recognizing the implications of all this, said with consternation and surprise: "Why, these people all know each other!"

The Establishment is linked not only by formal and informal ties but also by common backgrounds. Most members of the current Establishment are lineal and, according to their critics, spiritual descendants of house slaves and the free Negro elite. Not a few sprang from the black Puritan class which placed a high premium on respectability, responsibility and the middle-class values of thrift, sobriety and steadiness. Almost all of them were marked, for ill or good, by strong men and women who desperately, almost fanatically, dedicated themselves to proving—to themselves and to others—that they were not Negroes.

A common educational background also links the power structure. A significantly large percentage of top-level leadership has come from Ivy League colleges. Many more, however, came from a handful of Negro colleges which form a sub-Ivy League league. Howard University, for example, has served as a kind of post-graduate school for Harvard postgraduates. The number of Negro leaders who studied or taught at Howard (Bunche, Hastie, Thurgood Marshall, Charles E. Thompson, James Nabrit, Carl Murphy), is impressive. From these men came some of the Establishment's best thinking—pro and con. The successful legal campaign was mapped at Howard. The pioneer thinking on nonviolence came largely from Howard (Mordecai Johnson, James Farmer, Howard Thurman, W. S. Nelson). And the thinking for several beyond-the-Establishment organizations (the National Negro Congress, the Negro Sanhedrin) was hammered out there.

Atlanta and Nashville have been equally important as Establishment nurseries. The Southern branch of the Ivy League consists of Atlanta University (James Weldon Johnson, Walter White), Virginia Union (Eugene Kinckle Jones), Lincoln (Thurgood Marshall), Morehouse (Martin Luther King, Jr., James Nabrit, Jr., Mordecai Johnson) and Fisk (W. E. B. Du Bois, J. Finley Wilson, Charles Wesley).

The black Puritan background, the tutelage of white Puritans in New South missionary schools and New England universities, the proving of self and race against the standards of white power, the postgraduate training in and around Howard, Fisk, Morehouse and the leadership factories of Chicago, New York, and Washington: this was the common womb from which came men imbued with a stern sense of duty and responsibility, men driven and set apart, tragically separated from their white peers who patronized them and the Negro masses whom they patronized. This background, plus Du Bois' ideology of the Talented Tenth, sent forth leaders with a rather aristocratic and not altogether realistic concept of *noblesse oblige*—men who felt they were responsible for the masses and discharged that responsibility at a safe distance.

There was a mark on the brow of such men.

By the mark they recognized each other and excluded interlopers. In their time, and in their place, they made important contributions. It was not their fault, really, that they were products of their time and their place. It was not their fault—or was it, really?—that they learned caution with duty, that they learned to value order and respectability in the same places that taught them the desirability and the inevitability of social change. They were, on the whole, a remarkable lot. Though not rebels themselves, they tilled the ground and prepared the way for the bitter harvest.

For many years, this elite of family, education, property and, yes, color, was, in part, an interlocked directorate composed of several large families tied together by marriage and a larger group who stood in candidacy for power—and marriage.

There are indications that the Establishment is

losing some of its caste and color flavor. Despite in-group mating and a certain snobbishness based on status and color, the Establishment has always been open to talent backed by money and/or organization and, if possible, respectability. Within recent years, new members have entered the group by marriage and accomplishment. The bumper crop of new doctors and professional men with status and money has also changed the contours of the Establishment. More important still is the expanding middle class which makes it difficult to tell, without a scoreboard, where the Establishment ends and the commons begin.

Even more important as a factor in the waning influence of the Establishment is the revolt of the masses. Asa Philip Randolph opened a Pandora's box of mass participation when he called laborers and maids to the barricades in the forties. There is considerable evidence that the Establishment was scandalized. But since the process was unstoppable, the Establishment wisely joined the movement and pushed it forward.

The postwar world, which called off all bets, has shaken the Establishment to its foundation. Having fought off one challenge in the Garvey movement of the twenties, the Establishment found itself face to face with another mass-based black nationalist movement, the Nation of Islam. In this same period, there was a complete revolution in mass communication, a revolution that bewildered the Establishment and almost isolated it. In the void stepped John H. Johnson, an inventive Chicagoan who rose to the top ranks of the coalition Establishment with a new kind of journalism.

There were other changes: the shifting of the center of gravity from New York to Atlanta in the wake of the Montgomery boycott and the sit-ins and the emergence of the Negro student as a social force. The net result of these changes was a new correlation of forces in which a few ragged students could make decisions and carry them out without the "advise and consent" of the Establishment in faraway New York.

Then, in the sixties, the Establishment was called upon to face a long-suppressed issue: the growing chasm between it and the masses. Urban renewal, more than any other issue, made the Negro power structure face the fact that what is good for the Negro real estate broker or the Negro millionaire is not necessarily good for the Negro laborer or the maid on relief. A variety of issues in every big city, issues revolving around poverty and middle-classness or the lack of it, has called into question the good faith of the Establishment.

It would be a mistake to conclude from all this that the Establishment is dead. Far from it. With the resiliency that has marked it for more than fifty years, the group has grafted the new onto the old. New men with new power have been accepted by the *curia*—but the *curia* has, so far, failed to ask itself the ancient questions about new wine and old bottles. These questions are pushing the new men of power in quite a different direction. A new Establishment has sprung up around the core groups of the Southern Christian Leadership Conference, the

Student Nonviolent Coordinating Committee, the Congress of Racial Equality and the Negro American Labor League.

The new organizations are tapping new sources of Negro and white expressiveness. Radicals, pacifists, intellectuals, rebels, nonconformists—Negro and white—are finding niches in the new organizations. Among the persons who have served on the governing boards of the new organizations are Harry Belafonte (SNCC), Ella Baker (SNCC), Rev. C. K. Steele (SCLC and CORE Advisory Committee), Howard Thurman (CORE Advisory Committee), James Baldwin (CORE Advisory Committee) and L. D. Reddick (SCLC Historian).

Interestingly though, the new men of power are weaving yet another interlocking directorate. Rev. Fred Shuttlesworth, the president of the Alabama Conference of Human Rights, is secretary of SCLC. King himself and many of his aides and supporters flit in and out of CORE, the Fellowship of Reconciliation and other organizations.

An analysis of the governing boards of the old and new organizations reveals two different layers of support. With few exceptions, members of the old organizations are not members of the governing or advisory boards of the new organizations. Among the interesting exceptions are James B. Carey, Allan Knight Chalmers, Earl B. Dickerson, A. Philip Randolph, Ira De A. Reid, Walter Reuther, Hobson Reynolds, Jackie Robinson, and Bishop W. J. Walls.

The Establishment exists today as an uneasy coalition of old patriarchs, new men of power and rebels. But it still wields force as an independent power in the Negro world. Its continuing power and influence were evident in the March on Washington where Establishment men moderated and mitigated explosive forces and militant men.

The Establishment still lives, but it operates in a different climate. Establishment men grew up in a world where simple people acquiesced in the decisions of their betters. Now suddenly all that has changed. Policy is made now in the full glare of kleig lights with intellectuals, students and a comedian (Dick Gregory) looking over the policy-makers' shoulders.

Having survived Marcus Garvey in the twenties, black Lenins in the thirties, and Asa Philip Randolph in the forties, the Establishment is waiting now for the next turn of the wheel. The only thing wrong with this calculation is that the name of the game has changed. The young students and, behind them, the young black nationalists are playing for keeps. When a game or historical process reaches that point, as French conservatives and American Tories discovered, Establishment men who refuse to bet lose all the time.

Almost everyone knows that the white power structure is threatened by the Negro rebellion. What is not noted often enough is that Negro men of power are also on trial, not for the decisions they made but for the decisions they did not make, not for the battles they lost but for the battles they did not fight.

III
ETHOS:

Voices from the Cave

Robert Hutchins expressed dissatisfaction once with Negro grammar and American smugness. Too many Negroes, he wrote, tell us: "We want what you have." It seemed to Hutchins that the sentence should read: "You shouldn't want what you have."

The sharpest thrust, the most creative strain, of the Negro rebellion is now saying to us: "You shouldn't want what you have."

From the vanguard of the rebellion—from artists and writers in the North and students and rebels in the South—comes a message of renewal and regeneration. The message, to be sure, does not come from all Negroes; important segments of the Negro community still want what we have. But an increasingly large number of Negroes—the most creative part of the rebellion—are perceiving that what we have is not what we want and that what we are is not what we were intended to be.

The Negro rebellion, then, is a cultural as well as a social upheaval. Some demonstrators are marching for a place in the Establishment, but some are marching to express a vision that Establishments must be transcended in the direction of more expressive forms of human organization. The authentic rebels are not demonstrating for something they lack but for something they have and the feeling is growing that what they have is what America lacks. The old Negro spiritual expresses their yearning:

> *My soul wants something*
> *That's new, that's new.*

Integration and transformation: these two themes are at the heart of the rebellion which holds enormous possibilities for all Americans. For if the rebellion fulfills itself it will stimulate our creativity which only comes from diversity; it will relieve the drab sameness of our middle-class minds and our middle-class neighborhoods; it will give us an America more concerned about the claims of human personality and less concerned about color and machines.

The rebellion, in short, cuts to the bone of the deepest problems in American Culture. And American culture, in responding to the rebellion, will change—in one direction or another. Camus said once that the secret of Europe was that it no longer loved life. Before too many years have passed, America is going to have to make a decision: either for or against life.

This is the core meaning of the Negro rebellion which tells us that we can be better than we are, which tells us that we are a bridge to a better and unknown world and that we must cross that bridge or say goodbye forever to democracy and the American Dream.

The implications of all this are immense. The Negro has always been a creative ferment in American life. But we come now in our national life to the *conscious Negro,* the Negro as his own mythologist, a mythologist who not only creates myths about himself but also, and more importantly, about us.

We can note, in passing, the subtle change this has wrought in American life: the pressure of the black student rebel image on the internal dynamics of white students, and the extraordinary fascination of the Baldwin image or the Miles Davis image for white Americans who no longer find food for thought or action in the mainstream tradition—not to mention the large influence of the Negro as "vitality image" on a civilization dimly aware of its lack of both vitality and color.

Because of our generic bad faith, because of our adroitness in turning the tables and accusing our victims of racism, inauthentic Negroes shy away from this controversial area. In so doing, in reacting rather than acting, they murder the black foetus in their own hearts and play into the hands of their enemies. If they point timidly to the contributions of Negro Americans, contributions stemming not from race but from special experiences, they are accused of racism. But if they remain silent, the contributions of Negroes are appropriated and they are scorned as parasites who come empty handed to meetings of give and take. Let us have done with this spiritual swindle. Millions of American Negroes—I among them—are determined to express themselves directly, without a prior check with the white Other; they are determined to act and not to react with a full awareness of the Negro's essential American-ness and all that implies.

The Negro shares the same basic culture as all other Americans and he is moulded, more or less, by the same forces. But the Negro is also a Negro which means that he is, by definition, excluded from full participation in the life of our society. The Negro—and this is the key point—is a product, an elaboration of American society. His basic culture, his basic responses are American and Western. Whatever differences we observe between Negroes and other Americans are a result of one fact: the Negro's integration into American life was abruptly and artificially stopped at a point in time and he has not been permitted since then to blend into his environment in a natural way. In this sense and in this sense only can we speak of a Negro subculture. Identified as a Negro, treated as Negro, provided with Negro interests, forced, whether he wills or no, to live in Negro communities, to think, love, buy and breathe as a Negro, the Negro comes in time to see himself as a Negro. Invented by American civilization, he comes, in time, to invent himself and to imagine creatively his face.

During the protracted pains of his birth, the Negro underwent abnormal amounts of stress and strain and he responded with deep and elemental reactions that were deposited in the protoplasm of the Negro folk tradition. And it is this tradition that the Negro mythologist affirms as valid and meaningful for all men.

The tradition is the distillation of the long and

painful history of black men in a hostile environment and it bears the marks of a brutal struggle for survival. In the course of this struggle, the Negro went down to the doors of hell, knew cowardice in himself and in others and experienced the bottomless cruelty of man. He was stripped, literally stripped, of every prop and every defense.

> *I was way down yonder by myself*
> *And I couldn't hear nobody pray.*

Down *there*, at the bottom of himself, the Negro earned the right to speak of man and for man. What he saw, in the place where nobody was praying, what he dreamed and thought, speaks to us today in the Negro folk tradition. The tradition, in the beginning, was not sharply separated into sacred and secular strains; and the tradition and the Negro who bears that tradition cannot be understood without holding these two contradictory and yet complementary strains—sacred/secular—together in one's mind. This is, I think, the essential genius of the Negro tradition which did not and does not recognize the Platonic-Puritan dichotomies of good-bad, white-black, God-devil, body-mind. This has caused no end of misunderstanding, even among Negro mythologists who elaborate a blues mystique as opposed, say, to a spiritual mystique. The Negro tradition, read right, recognizes no such dichotomy. The blues are the spirituals, good is bad, God is the devil and every day is Saturday. The essence of the tradition is the extraordinary tension between the poles of pain and joy, agony and ecstasy, good and bad, Sunday and Saturday. One can, for convenience, separate the tradition into Saturdays (blues) and Sundays (spirituals). But it is necessary to remember that the blues and the spirituals are not two different things. They are two sides of the same coin, two banks, as it were, defining the same stream.

What is lacking in most white interpretations of Negro reality is a full-bodied evocation of the entire spectrum. By seizing on one element to the exclusion of the other, by making an artificial separation of Saturdays and Sundays, white interpreters and white imitators of the Negro deform themselves and the total ensemble of the Negro tradition which stands or falls as a bloc.

There are definite affinities between the core concepts of the Negro tradition and Zen Buddhism, existentialism and certain modern movements in physics and psychotherapy. The creators of this great tradition respected the cutting edge of life; they understood that good and evil, creative and destructive, wise and foolish, up and down, were inseparable polarities of existence.

> *Sometimes I'm up*
> *Sometimes I'm down*
> *Oh, yes, Lord.*

This attitude, so un-Anglo Saxon in its balance and complexity, permeates the whole of the Negro tradition which looks life full in the face and smiles at "the fast black train" of death. This comes out in the blues which speak of the agony of life and of the possibility of transcending it by sheer toughness of spirit.

> *I got the blues*
> *But I'm too damned mean to cry.*

It comes out in the spirituals which speak of exile and homelessness and of total and immediate responsibility in the bosom of one's aloneness.

> *I went to the rock*
> *To hide my face*
> *The rock cried out*
> *No hiding place.*

It comes out in the tougher and more cynical devil songs which were created by the vast majority of slaves who were non-, if not, anti-Christian and who expressed themselves in obscene, amoral, beyond atheism plaints that elucidated a vision of existential absurdity.

> *Our father, who is in heaven*
> *White man owe eleven and pay me seven,*
> *Thy kingdom come, thy will be done,*
> *And if I hadn't took that, I wouldn't had none.*

The extraordinary thing here is the quiet understatement. The post-Civil War hipster did not complain; he did not whine; he did not accept—he merely stated a situation involving himself, the white man, and God and in stating that situation with such chilling objectivity he judged not only himself and the white man but also God.

The overemphasis on the spirituals and their adoption by polite society has obscured this hidden dimension in the tradition. The devil strain, which persists today in the products of the non-religious underclass, reminds us afresh of the extraordinary complexity of a tradition which always and everywhere affirms the unity of life: no black without white, no joy without pain, no life without death.

Deliciously and baldly human in an artificial and hypocritical world, the Negro folk tradition confronts life in the raw, celebrates the here and now and takes no thought of tomorrow. The songs of the ethos and its dances affirm that which God made, the body; and they say that that which God made was good. Flowing out of this radical affirmation of the facticity of flesh is a healthy respect for the sacredness of sex as communion and creation.

> *Make it soft and low*
> *Make it Baby soft and low*
> *If you feel like layin' down, Baby*
> *With me on the floor.*

Accepting all that God accepts, the tradition is tolerant of everything except right angles of the spirit. The pretender, the imposter, the striver, the strainer, the "square" are condemned. Being is recommended instead of seeming, the natural response instead of the contrived one. The tradition urges men to turn themselves loose, to give themselves up to spontaneity and improvisation. It urges them to dance not only with the feet but with the ears, the eyes, the shoulders, the buttocks, the spirit, the soul.

The whole corpus of the tradition, in fact, is compressed into the folk myth of *Soul*, the American counterpart of the African *Negritude*, a distinct quality of Negro-ness growing out of the Negro's experience and not his genes. *Soul* is a metaphorical evocation of Negro being as expressed in the Negro tradition. It is the feeling with which an artist invests his creation, the style with which a man lives his life. It is, above all, the spirit rather than the letter: a certain way of feeling, a certain way of expressing oneself, a certain way of being. To paraphrase Sartre, *Soul* is the Negro's antithesis (black) to America's thesis (white), a confrontation of spirits that could and should lead to a higher synthesis of the two.

Our primary interest here is not in the metaphorical myth of *Soul*, nor in particular manifestations of the tradition it invokes. What holds our attention is the total ensemble and the values undergirding it: a relaxed and noncompetitive approach to being, a complex acceptance of the contradictions of life, a buoyant sadness, a passionate spontaneity, and a gay sorrow.

From the womb of this non-Puritan, nonmachine, nonexploitative tradition have come insights, values and attitudes that have changed the face of America. The tradition is very definitely nonmachine, but it is not antimachine; it simply recognizes that machines are generative power and not soul, instruments and not ends. It is this insight which draws us to the Harlems of the mind. Time and time again, we have turned to the Negro tradition as a tonic for the sickness of our souls. The hip generation of today is merely imitating the Flappers of the twenties who sought the Garden of Eden in the Harlems of yesterday. The Garden of Eden is not in Harlem; but it is a psychological fact of prime importance that we believe, have always believed, that it is there—or nearby. What is in Harlem, really—and Harlem is not a place but a region of our minds—is a sundered part of ourselves. But it is this, precisely, that we are fleeing; and, fleeing, we find neither ourselves nor the Negro nor freedom.

The flight to Harlem is, in part, a projection of our bad faith, of a desire to believe that the Negro has, after all, gotten something out of his degradation. But there is, I believe, a deeper and truer motivation: an obsessive fear that perhaps we have lost something by our complicity in degradation.

Standing in the no man's land between white adult culture and the Negro subculture, which is, in part, the culture of the white young, the Negro as mythologist verifies the losses of the oppressor and asserts the validity of insights paid for by the blood of men and women who gained nothing from oppression but learned a great deal in the transcendence of that oppression. As an apostle of wholeness, the Negro mythologist points the way to a natural and harmonious blending of the deepest insights of both the dominant white culture and the Negro subculture. Bearing the marks of both cultures, he fleshes out, in his androgyny, the hoped-for synthesis. In his person, he tells us, louder than a thousand trumpets, that we are already one and that what we lack is a consciousness, an awareness, of that fact.

The architect of this insight, the advance guard of the movement for renewal, is the conscious Negro, the Negro who accepts the implications and meaning of his own experience, who accepts that experience and wills himself and it into the mainstream as conscious agents of change. Plunging into the heart of the Negro tradition, the conscious Negro holds up a mirror to the Negro and the white man and reveals them to themselves as victims and creators of each other.

The conscious Negro, as artist and demonstrator, takes his stand within the context of his tradition and projects himself outwardly with the full knowledge that a man is most human when he is most himself. At a recent conference of writers and artists, one of scores called to debate the question of the Negro writer and his roots, Ossie Davis, the playwright and actor, expressed this thrust with a Langston Hughes poem:

> *My old mule*
> *Got a grin on his face;*
> *He been a mule so long*
> *He forgot about his race.*
> *Now, I'm like that mule*
> *Black, and don't give a damn*
> *You got to take me like I am.*

There is a radical conception at work in this affirmation, a conception that reflects an equally radical alteration in the stance of the Negro who no longer, generally speaking, believes that white is right. The Negro, in the person of his most gifted members, is moving within himself and taking a more objective stance toward American culture. He is beginning to re-define himself and, of necessity, to re-define the white man.

For the old especially, this is a desperately serious business, an attempt to grasp from the white man's books and his images and his myths a lost and devalued part of themselves. What Negroes are trying to do, at bottom, is to wrest the Negro image from white control. The Negro image in America is basically a contrast conception, one part of the familiar dichotomies of good-evil, clean-dirty, white-black. In the past, some Negroes attempted to define themselves by becoming counter-contrast conceptions, by becoming, in short, opposite Negroes, opposite, that is, to what white men said Negroes were. This strategy is now being abandoned by writers and artists who say that white Americans can no longer tell them who they are and where they came from and where they should want to go. Refusing to be bound by the *white man's definitions*, they contend that the Negro is not a white man with black skin but simply a man, undefined, unpredictable, free. As for the white men, they insist that he, too, is a bridge, a promise, a being to be transcended.

Seen within the context of the Negro rebellion, this is an act of affirmation, a creative leap into being, a leap directly related to the crisis of culture in the heart of America and, indeed, in the heart of the Western world. At its crudest, it is the simple assertion that black is right. At its highest, it is the affirmation of the validity of nonwhite traditions and nonwhite values as complements to white traditions and white values. However expressed, it is the affirmation of the old truth that a man must be at home somewhere before he can create a home anywhere.

It is the function of free men to question prevailing mythologies. It is their duty to tell us what time it is historically. By questioning the deception of appearances, by analyzing their own private hells and by becoming their own mythologists, Negro artists and writers are forcing us to face an unpalatable fact.

Less than one hundred years ago, Neitzsche announced to a startled world that God was dead. Religion apart, he was announcing a psychological fact, the death of God in the heart of his contemporaries. What we have to deal with today is a psychological fact of a similar dimension. *The white man is dead.* He died at Auschwitz and Buchenwald. He died at Hiroshima. He died in Montgomery and Birmingham and Little Rock. *The white man is dead.* Men with pale skins still live. But the *idea* of a man with a certain color skin and a mandate from God to order and regulate the lives of men with darker skins: that idea is dead—in Panama and in Kenya, in Milwaukee and in Mississippi. We no longer live in a world controlled by that idea, though some people, Negroes and whites, have not read the obituary notices. The mourners are as yet only intellectuals and little children, Negroes and whites. But the idea is spreading and it shows up in areas beyond intellection—in the flight of Picasso and other modernists to Benin and Ife, a fact that indicated beyond doubt that what we call the tradition, the Greco-Roman, Anglo-Teuton tradition, no longer had the power to move its most creative members. We deal gingerly with the fact in America. We have only to remember the spate of essays on the white Negro, the adoption of hip postures by the avant-garde and the fact, to paraphrase Leslie Fiedler, that Americans now spend their childhood as imaginary Indians, their adolescence as imaginary Negroes and their adulthood as imaginary whites.

In the person of the conscious Negro, America comes hard up against a new fact: the color of the world has changed. With that change, a terrifying freedom becomes the burden of all men, especially those men who were tyrannized for so long by a concept that cruelly twisted and warped the inner contours of their minds. If white men come forward now to claim their own freedom and individuality, if they abandon their hard-fought trenches and come out into the open, we will have an extraordinary renaissance not only in the arts but in our daily lives.

A similar burden assails Negroes who have been, to borrow Plato's image, sitting chained for four hundred years in a cave with their backs to the sun. White men told them for four hundred years that they were the shadows they saw on the wall. The Negro is breaking his chains now and is turning around to face the fire of the sun. He has not yet opened his eyes; he may, in fact, never open his eyes. Still, the possibility is there. What will he say when he sees himself and others in the lucidity of pure light? What will he write? What will he think? What will he say about us and about himself? We do not know. But we can say, I think, that if the Negro really opens his eyes the culture of America will be widened, deepened and strengthened by the insights, anguish and passion of the Negro soul.

No Negro artist, so far, has plumbed the depth and passion of the Negro experience. No writer, so far, has fingered pain and dread with the exquisite agony of a Billie Holiday. No Negro poet, no philosopher or pundit has said as much about the human condition as Charlie Parker or Bessie Smith. Negro letters still awaits a man who will take his stand within the context of Negro experience and project himself outwardly in a comment on the human condition. Negro philosophy still awaits its Sartre; Negro literature still awaits its Kafka; Harlem still awaits a Haman.

James Baldwin said once that there has not yet arrived a sensibility sufficiently tough to make the Negro experience articulate. The man of the future has not yet arrived; but he is coming. Baldwin himself is a harbinger of a black and white tomorrow. But there are many lesser-known men in the cultural hothouses of Detroit, Chicago, New York, and San Francisco. More important still are the young rebels on the firing line in Mississippi, Alabama, and Georgia; more important because they act, whereas the writers and artists merely talk. Still, the talk is important. In poetry and in prose, in magazines like *Negro Digest, Dasein* and *Umbra,* young artists, writers and sociologists are expressing a newfound pride in being black. They are saying to America that the long white solo is over and that a dialogue of a black I and a white Thou must now begin, a dialogue between two individuals confronting each other in all their concretion and facticity, in community, if possible, but in conflict, if necessary.

Two decades ago Von Keyserling said that Negro Americans would probably make America's greatest cultural contribution. If, twenty years later, this prediction has not come to pass, be not dismayed. There are many mysteries in the womb of time, and the wheel of fate is turning.

IV

PASSION:

A Certain Dark Joy

TODAY, MORE THAN EVER, we need to remember how much we owe the Negro.

If, as Eric Williams said, the Negro is today the white man's problem, he was in the beginning the only solution to that problem.

The crisis of the hour calls us to a remembrance of beginnings and a prevision of endings. It calls us, above all else, to a remembrance of the hot black fire Negroes breathed into the snowy reaches of our souls.

There is a rather romantic notion abroad that white men give without receiving. But culture is nothing if not a dialogue. The white man has influenced the Negro, particularly in the area of technique, but the Negro has had a comparable influence on the white man, particularly in the area of sensibility. In *The Mind of the South*, W. J. Cash spoke of the "tyranny" of the Negro over the customs and habits of white Southerners. "Negro," he said, "entered into white man as profoundly as white man entered into Negro—subtly influencing every gesture, every word, every emotion and idea, every attitude." Negro entered into white man not only in the South but also in the North. Every arena of American life—politics, labor, education, religion, art, recreation—has been greatly conditioned by the pervasive presence of the Negro; and every American bears on his body or, deeper, in his soul the mark of fire of the Negro.

Spiritually, we are all Negroes. In our nonmachine life, we are all imitators of the Negro who has always been a ferment in the rather colorless amalgam of American life. When C. J. Jung, the great psychologist, visited America, he was astonished by the mark of the Negro. "The first thing which attracted my attention," he was quoted as saying, "was the influence of the Negro, an obviously psychological influence regardless of any mixture of blood." Jung went on to say that the influence of the Negro was apparent in the walking, laughing, dancing, singing and even the praying of white Americans. What Jung was trying to say—and we didn't need him to tell us this—was that the Negro is deep in the psyche and soma of America. His roots are deeper than the Puritan's. Negro men and women came here long before the Mayflower and they cleared the forests, drained the swamps and cultivated the grain. The wealth of this country was founded on what Abraham Lincoln called "the 250 years of unrequited toil" of Negro men and women. From the muted wail of slaves going in chains to American plantations came the gold that made capitalism possible; from black brawn came tobacco; from black blood, white sugar.

Had there been no Negroes here, *had there*

been no darkness at all, this would be a pale and a lonely land.

No Negroes?

What would we sing?

No darkness?

What would we dance?

No blackness?

What would we fear? How would we experience the boundaries and the whiteness of our lives?

This is not now, nor has it ever been, a white country. More than ever today, we need to remember the contributions of Negroes, and the black and white roots in the subsoil of our lives. For make no mistake about it: We cannot understand ourselves if we do not understand the Negro and what he has dreamed in this country. Or to put it another way: We cannot understand ourselves until we understand the symbolic darkness within and the literal darkness without.

America would not have been America without the Negro and America cannot become America until it confronts not only the Negro but the gifts the Negro bears. What is required now is an act of the spirit. We must abandon our shallow trenches and confront each other as coinheritors of a common land, which is to say that we must meet and know each other as brothers in a marriage of visions, as coconspirators in the making of a dream, as fellow passengers on a journey into the unknown.

It was from out of the unknown that the Negro came, bringing with him the gift of the sun. Billowing out of the slave ships and the embryonic Harlems of the plantations was the sun of a fierce and irresistible will to life. And the sun within the Negro sustained him and made him the white man's greatest collaborator in the taking of the land. *The Negro endured:* let us begin with that contribution. By the simple act of survival, the Negro made an inestimable contribution to his posterity and to his native land. When Europeans settled in the West Indies, whole groups of people disappeared from the face of the earth, leaving nothing behind but a few bones and artifacts. In other places and in other climes, brown and red men drank the white man's whiskey, read his Bible, became demoralized and wasted away into nothingness. The Negro drank the white man's whiskey, read his Bible, did his work—and his tribe increased. He descended into the hell of slavery, was denied books, pencil and paper, was denied the sanctity of marriage—was crucified, in fact, and rose again some three hundred years later in Chicago and Harlem and Atlanta and Washington. *The Negro endured.*

There is hope in the Negro's incredible vitality— hope and promise and danger. The Negro population of our fifteen largest metropolitan areas—the urban heart of America—is growing hour by hour. So is the ghetto; so is the Negro's impatience, frustration and alienation. Take Chicago, for example. There are almost nine hundred thousand Negroes in Chicago. Soon there will be a million or more. The white population is decreasing; *it has decreased every year since 1930.* If Negroes are not integrated into the total fabric of the community, if the ghetto is not smashed, if the white panic continues, Chicago—the big-talking, hog-butchering, money-making Chicago of Sandburg and Dreiser and Wright—will become a predominantly Negro city.

The men who run Chicago and other metropolitan areas are trying frantically to roll back the tide with urban renewal and other finger-in-the-dike plans. But they are attempting, as one writer put it, to cure a cancer with dandruff remover. Week by week, day by day, the glacier-like ghetto spreads. Every week more than two hundred housing units change from white to Negro occupancy. The Negroes move in, the whites move out. There are hard words, broken windows, fights, bombs. Some whites run to the suburbs, others move further south or west where months or years later they meet Negroes and pick up and run again. This has been going on now for years, but it cannot go on forever. Chicago and other metropolitan areas are fast approaching Joe Louis' iron law of runmanship: whites can run, but they cannot hide forever. Arithmetic, time, the Fourteenth Amendment, the spirit of the age, the Negro birthrate and the Illinois Central Railroad are against them.

Ten years from now or twenty years from now, when Negroes comprise from one-third to more than one-half of the population of our major cities, a bill is coming due. Sooner or later, in a good season or a bad season, the Commonwealth is going to have to decide between the American idea or Fascism.

Frederick Douglass, the great Negro abolitionist, said it one hundred and thirteen years ago. *"We are here*, and here we are likely to be. To imagine that we shall ever be eradicated is absurd and ridiculous. We can be remodified, changed, and assimilated, but never extinguished. We repeat, therefore, that *we are here*, and that this is *our country*. . . . We shall neither die out, nor be driven out; but shall go with this people, either as a testimony against them, or as an evidence in their favor throughout their generations."

By going "with this people," Negroes have played a large role in the survival of America. Hundreds of thousands of Negroes, from Bunker Hill to Vietnam, have died for an idea that was not real in their own lives. Has any other people in any other age had such faith and hope—and received so little charity? When Lincoln spoke of "the mystic chords of memory, stretching from every battlefield and patriot grave, to every living heart and hearth-stone," the words had meaning in the ghetto. Negro men and women signed the Declaration of Independence with the blood of their spirit. Some five thousand Negro soldiers fought in the Revolutionary War and more than one hundred and eighty thousand fought for the Union and the freedom of their fellow men in the Civil War.

The "mystic chords of memory" and the graves of black patriots stretch from Valley Forge to the banks of the Rhine. When General Putnam said, "Don't shoot until you see the white of their eyes," black men were there. When Admiral Farragut said, "Damn the torpedoes full speed ahead," John Lawson was in earshot and his gallantry won him a Congressional Medal of Honor. When Major Pitcairn stormed up Bunker Hill and said, "The day is ours," Peter Salem shot straight and true.

Roscoe Jamison, the Negro poet, saw the long black lines marching off to make the world safe for democracy and cried out in anguish:

> *These truly are the Brave,*
> *These men who cast aside*
> *Old memories to walk the blood-stained pave*
> *Of Sacrifice, joining the solemn tide*
> *That moves away, to suffer and to die*
> *For Freedom—when their own is yet denied!*
> *O Pride! O Prejudice! When they pass you by,*
> *Hail them, the Brave, for you now crucified!*

It is of freedom that the Negro speaks and it has been his privilege and his responsibility to remind us of the blood of our birth. By continually raising the cry of freedom, the Negro has had an enormous impact on the American idea of democracy. It can be said, in fact, that the whole history of American democracy is a series of approaches to and retreats from Negro reality.

In this struggle, the Negro has been far from passive. Charles Hamilton Houston, Thurgood Marshall and a long line of Negro lawyers have virtually rewritten the constitutional law of this land. Because of the Marshalls and the Martin Luther Kings, the rights of all men are more secure today.

By an extraordinary default, white Americans have lost all claims to exclusive identification with the deepest insights of their tradition. The torch of freedom has passed, ironically, from the sons of the masters to the sons of the slaves. Born into mission, ordained, as it were, from birth as an advocate of freedom, the Negro is the only American who consistently makes an issue of democracy at home. And so long as he lives we will not be able to forget the revolution of our birth.

The Negro has played a modest but nonetheless important role as a conservator of human values. He has been a hewer of water here, but he has also been a hewer of the human spirit. Negro expressiveness began early. In 1761, a slim black girl named Phillis Wheatly came to America in a slave ship. Within twelve months, she was writing fluent English; within twelve years, she was an internationally-known poet. In 1773, this "black daughter of the sun" brought out a volume of poems that was the second book published by an American woman. This was in an age, incidentally, when few white women—or white men for that matter—read books. In this same period, Benjamin Banneker, a free Negro of Maryland, distinguished himself as an astronomer, almanac-maker, surveyor, botanist, zoologist and philosopher. Banneker also experimented with the velocity of sound waves, wrote a dissertation on bees and helped to lay out the city of Washington, D.C.

Since Appomattox, Negro scientists and inventors have received more than five thousand patents, ranging from machine guns and electronic devices to machines for utilizing atomic energy. When Americans pick up a telephone, buy a pair of shoes or ride a railroad, they are paying tribute to the genius of both Negro and white Americans, to Granville

T. Woods, for example, who invented a telephone transmitter that American Bell bought and Jan E. Matzeliger who revolutionized the shoe industry with a machine for attaching soles to shoes.

The millions of Americans who have been blinded by glaucoma, the millions of Americans whose lives have been saved by blood plasma should thank God the Negroes came this way. They should give thanks for Dr. Percy Julian who made a successful synthesis of the drug Physostigmine and Dr. Charles Drew who perfected the blood plasma technique that saved the lives of so many white Americans in World War II. Americans are also indebted to George Washington Carver who revolutionized Southern agriculture with his research on pecans, peanuts and sweet potatoes; Dr. Daniel Hale Williams who made what was probably the first successful operation on the human heart; Dr. Edward L. Harris, a leading authority on rocket and jet fuels; and Luther Prince who made a key contribution in the development of an automatic brain for the X-15, America's first rocket ship.

America would not have been America without the contributions of these and other Negro men and women, without Paul Laurence Dunbar, Langston Hughes, and Gwendolyn Brooks in poetry; Richard Wright, Ralph Ellison, and James Baldwin in letters; James Bland, W. C. Handy, Louis Armstrong, Duke Ellington, and Charlie Parker in music; Paul Robeson, Bert Williams, and Bill Robinson in the theater; W. E. B. Du Bois, and Carter G. Woodson in the realm of ideas; Joe Louis, Jessie Owens, Wilt Chamberlain, and Willie Mays in sports; and Robert Weaver and Ralph J. Bunche in public affairs.

In addition to the many individual contributions, Negroes have given America the blind fire of their faith. Negroes were brought to America, enslaved and taught the word of Jesus. Through some miracle no man can explain, some of the slaves believed. In the black pews and the Jim Crow galleries, in the sharecroppers' cabins and the concrete ghettoes, some Negroes caught a glimpse of the real meaning and substance of primitive Christianity and their lighted torch has become a new center of diffusion giving light to all who come within the range of its radiance.

Going straight to the heart of the matter, the Negro slave gave central importance to that which Christians have been fleeing for almost two thousand years: the cross.

Were you there when they crucified my Lord?
Were you there when they nailed him to the tree?
Oh, sometimes, it causes me to tremble, tremble,
    tremble.

In this question, one of the deepest utterances on the crucifixion in the whole literature of the Western world, time and space are annihilated and every man is made a witness and a betrayer of truth. The implication here is that the slave was *there*, that he knew something about Jesus that no man who did not stand with him, or near him, could possibly know.

A long time ago, when I was a little boy in Mississippi, my grandmother used to rock and sing that song. I was too young then to know what kind of troubles a black woman in Mississippi could have, but I remember the way she sang the song and I remember thinking then that the words were insufferably sad and insufferably beautiful. Looking back now, I think I know what she meant then: that she was *there*, that she knew—at the deepest level of her being—what it was like to be crucified on a cross between two thieves. And more: that there were some things in this world that were worth being crucified for.

My grandmother and her generation were perhaps the last living witnesses of a religious tradition that surged like billowing flames from the choir lofts and rickety benches of old Baptist and Methodist churches, of a tradition that dared to flesh out that without which religion is a mere Sunday morning game: the fatherhood of God and the brotherhood of man. The old men and women of this tradition could see the face of God nowhere in Mississippi or Alabama and yet they dared to dream that He was everywhere. Everything they could see—the ropes, the walls and the signs made by white Christians— told them the world was absurd and capricious at its core and yet they dared, out of a terrible and an eloquent hope, to bet on that which they could not see, saying to themselves, to their children, to the wind, to the mute sky that something—call it God, call it Mind, call it Spirit, call it what you will— that something higher than their masters or the white man was at work in history. In the face of overwhelming evidence to the contrary, in the face of lynchings, legalized robbery, institutionalized degradation, they dared to affirm the goodness and the greatness of man. What audacity! Not since Paul walked the road to Damascus, not since the Christian church was scandalous—and relevant—have men and women dreamed a dream of greater grandeur. And one can only hope that they were ushered at last into the presence of an old Jew who could say, out of the agony and the joy of His own life, that the dream they dreamed was true.

There cannot possibly be a Negro anywhere who does not carry somewhere deep within him the embers of that great fire. But we must understand, and quickly, that the faith of the grandmother or the grandfather is not the faith of the granddaughter or of the grandson. Too many people are dead in the coliseum, too many lies have been told for men to believe in the old way if, indeed, they find it possible to believe at all. The wheel of faith is turning in the ghetto and the fire is growing cold. The Negro cannot and will not stand forever in the wings offering the gifts of pain and passion and renewal.

The Negro religious tradition speaks to us for perhaps the last time in the Negro rebellion which came out of the pews and pulpits of the Negro church. The last embers of the faith glow in the hearts of Negro protestants who tramp the white and watchful streets singing the old spirituals and chanting the old hopes. What the Negro protestants seek, really, is a validation of *our* faith. And if they can force us to confront ourselves, if they can drag us, screaming and crying, into the presence of our cross, they will perform that miracle of which Toynbee and others dreamed, the transformation of the Christian Church and the transformation of Western life.

The great gift of the Negro religious tradition is inseparably related to the rhythms and melodies of the Negro folk idiom. No men born this side of the seas have worked closer to the aorta of the human spirit than Negro makers of meter and melody. The only original response Americans have made in this area came from despised and downtrodden Negroes in the ghettos and the slave shacks. Jazz, the spirituals, and the blues are recognized almost everywhere as unique American contributions to the arts. These gifts, which are part of the basic American vocabulary, are no longer racial. Our national art of dancing is an extension of Negro dancing, of the Charleston, the Black Bottom, the Lindy Hop, and the Twist. Our national popular music is a series of glosses and oftentimes distortions of the wails and the hollers and the cries of black bards.

You say—and I hear you saying—that these are minor contributions. But who is to say, really? By what standard are we to judge? Men cannot live without machines in the modern world but they assuredly cannot live by machines alone. In the long sight of history, it may be more important to influence the nonmachine aspects of a people's life than their technology. More than two hundred years ago, Andrew Fletcher said, "Give me the making of the popular songs of a nation and I care not who make its laws." Laws and songs apart, it is certain that the tempo of our lives has been altered permanently by the bitter honesty, the rhythmic complexity and the pulsations of freedom—physical, mental and spiritual freedom—that flow out of the best products of the Negro folk idiom.

There is still another seed in the Negro community that promises a bountiful harvest: the seed of a certain dark joy. With a tenacity that is somewhat frightening, with a resilience that is very beautiful, the Negro—the middle class excepted—has resisted the corrupting influence of money and machines at any price. In the direct circumstances, in fear and trembling, in blood and suffering, the Negro has retained a certain dark joy—a zest for life, a creative capacity for meeting adversity and transcending it—that is beautiful and meaningful. It was this, I think, that inspired that great poet, W. E. B. Du Bois, to say once that there was something strange and holy about the ghetto's Saturday night. Du Bois was not talking about race—nor am I—or a romanticized ghetto—nor am I. What Du Bois was trying to get at, I think, was the terrible aliveness of that night. He was talking not about Negroes but about life: good and bad, preachers and prostitutes, gin and champagne, tragedy and triumph, having and not having, giving and taking, losing and winning—Life.

Americans who have—generally speaking—externalized almost everything, who live by machines and die by them, who mortgage their souls for pieces of tin and split-level caves in middle-class hells; Americans who have lost the capacity for enjoying themselves and others, who are lonely and frightened and afraid—Americans could use some of that life-giving force.

For almost four hundred years, the Negro—again with distinguished exceptions—has resisted the demons that pursued the Puritans and the demons that pursue the sons of the Puritans. He is not afraid of sex and four-letter words—all exceptions freely admitted. And he knows the limitations, if not always the value, of money. He knows, as only saints and fanatics and children know, that it is sometimes better to spend money on candy or wine and that sometimes it is better to give it away entirely. I would not be misunderstood. I know the value—and the limitations—of money, and I know that Negroes need more money. Still, there must be a *via media* somewhere and it is the Negro's task to find it and show it to America. Black Puritans, who drool over America's Faustian obsession with money and power, do not seem to recognize that the essence of Faustianism is a deal involving not money or power but the soul. This is the central weakness of the black nationalist's posture. By following the oppressor in his worship of skin color, by following him in his lust for money and power, by following him in the denial of the brotherhood of man, the black nationalist practices that sincerest form of flattery: imitation. The black nationalist says: "The white man has been beastly: let us imitate him." It would be more logical to say: "The white man, generally speaking, has been beastly: let us—all of us, Negroes and whites—transcend him."

It is necessary, of course, for Negroes to appropriate and use the *instruments* of the strong if they are not to die or, what is worse, be continually humiliated. But a great deal more is required if one is not to become in the end what one deplored in the beginning, an oppressor or, at least, a mirrored image of an oppressor. In order to avoid that pitfall, one must transcend not only the oppressor but the values of oppression. To accept the boundaries of the given, to accept as valid only those ideals proven by the experiences of the oppressor is to doom oneself to social and spiritual sterility.

There is little or no hope for the Negro in this country if he continues to accept, uncritically and completely, the values and goals and ideals of his oppressors. To cite only one example: the Negro who accepts the ideal of blondness must, and inevitably does, hate himself. And again: the Negro who accepts completely the success and power ethic must also hate himself, for there is no defense for an unavenged defeat in a power ethic. Hence it is that some Negroes hate themselves and their history because their forefathers were *slaves* and not *slaveowners*.

At some point, we must ask ourselves where we are going and why and what is the price of admission. At some point, we must dare to ask the question of the lucid Neitzsche: "Not free from what, but free for what?" While there is still time, while the storm clouds are gathering, we ought to wrestle with that question.

"Not free from what, but free for what?"

A large number of Negroes—many of them Freedom Fighters—are attacking not only segregation but hypocrisy—Negro and white. They are asking not only for human dignity but for a society open to all of the creative possibilities in man. They are demanding integration but they are thinking beyond integration. These young people—may their tribe increase—are saying: "Not integration, but transformation."

I have not intended here to eulogize the virtues of Negroes. I believe all men are created equal and that Negroes are as bad—and as good—as other peoples. And yet, by the grace of God and the whip of history, Negroes, in the main, have not completely assimilated those values that are driving Western man to social and spiritual suicide: acquisitiveness, for example, numbness of heart and machine idolatry. To the extent that these things are foreign to the Negro's *experience,* to that extent the Negro is uniquely qualified to take the lead in recasting the human values of our civilization.

Having given so much, it is within the Negro's power to make this final gift to America: a society transformed by the spirit of compassion and creativity. He will make this gift, I think, when he accepts himself completely—his hair, his skin color, his nose formation, his emotions, his *everything*— and when he realizes that the Negro has as much to offer the white man as the white man has to offer the Negro.

Blood, sweat, tears, brains, brawn, and a certain dark joy: these are the gifts of the Negro to America. Freedom—freedom for both Negroes and whites —and a more abundant life: these are the blessings the Negro can bring to America if he keeps faith with himself and the long line of nameless men and women, the cooks, the maids, the cotton pickers, the millions of poor, faceless, anonymous Negroes who took the vilest punishment inflicted on a people in the Western world, who took it and survived, leaving an indelible message on the white marble of our souls: "The darkness is light enough."

V

TEA AND SYMPATHY:

Liberals and Other White Hopes

Who?

Who are our enemies and who are our friends?

For the Jew in Germany and the Jew in Scarsdale, for the African in Salisbury and the African in London, for the Negro in Birmingham and the Negro in New York City, there is only one question:

Who?

Who will harm and who will help?

Before bread can be earned and eaten, before love can be made, men who stand with their backs against the wall must answer that question. For various reasons, most of them eminently realistic, oppressed people have insisted, with disturbing unanimity, that it is impossible to be both a member of the oppressor class and a friend of the oppressed. This is, to be sure, an unrealistic postulate, a product of the sensitivity and subjectivity of downtrodden people. But let us face one harsh fact at the very beginning: no Jew was ever cremated, no Negro was ever lynched because he underestimated the passion and the perseverance of men who identified themselves as his friend.

White friends of the American Negro claim, with

some justification, that Negroes attack them with more heat than they attack declared enemies. This plaint runs like a thread through the history of oppression. For reasons no psychologist can really explain, oppressed people have always preferred a declared enemy to a false or, at least, an uncertain friend. Above all else, the strong man of the oppressed group prefers the open hate of a hateful man to the tea and sympathy of a timid man. It was noted in Europe, for example, that Jews wearing yellow stars preferred feigned indifference or open hostility rather than the embarrassed and timid and ineffectual approaches of men who wanted to *demonstrate* their tolerance. Considerations of style and taste apart, oppressed people have always considered it dangerous to encourage what the abolitionists called "halfness."

Because the half-friend is neither fish nor fowl, because he sides now with the oppressor and now with the oppressed, he commands the respect of neither the oppressor nor the oppressed. To sit on the fence when men are throwing rocks is neither a very safe nor a very effective public posture. With great foresight, Dante designated one of the lower places of hell for men who remained on the fence in a time of great moral crisis.

Oppressed people learn early that the problem of life is not the problem of evil but the problem of good. For this reason, they focus their fire on the *bona fides* of avowed friends. And in their heart of hearts they always answer the question of questions as Denmark Vesey, the great slave rebel, answered it: "He that is not for me, is against me."

What does all this mean within the context of the American situation where men are so close and yet so far apart that they dare not hate each other wholly and cannot love each other either wholly or in part?

Who are our enemies?

All those whose sins of omission and commission *practically* uphold a status quo where grown men hunger, children wither and old women cry. They are the enemy—and they are not all white.

And our friends?

No man can say. Friendship in a situation of oppression is friendship beyond situations of oppression. Friendship in such a situation is not a pledge; it is an *act*. It is an address of one's total being to the destruction of the situation of oppression. One can say that one is a friend of the oppressed, but one can only mean it by doing something about it, by tearing down and by building up. In the end, friendship for the oppressed can only be proven in an extreme situation where one is forced to choose —once, finally and for all—for either the oppressor or the oppressed. In this sense, friendship is *an act to the end*, an act that cannot be validated without an end or, at least, a beginning of an end.

But to speak of friends, to speak specifically of friends of the Negro, is, of necessity, to speak of enemies. For any man who identifies himself as a friend of the Negro identifies himself as the Negro's enemy. There is an insidious paternalism in that phrase that all the detergent in America cannot wash out. To be a friend of the Negro or of the Jew or of the native one must go beyond situations that create Negroes and Jews and natives.

To rephrase the question, then, who is *our*, who is man's, who is freedom's friend?

The white liberal answers; let us begin with him. The white liberal is a man who finds himself defined as a white man, as an oppressor, in short, and retreats in horror from that *designation*. But —and this is essential—he retreats only halfway, disavowing the title without giving up the privileges, tearing out, as it were, the table of contents and keeping the book. The fundamental trait of the white liberal is his desire to differentiate himself psychologically from white Americans on the issue of race. He wants to think and he wants others to think he is a man of brotherhood.

The white liberal talks brotherhood; he writes about it, prays for it, and honors it. But:

> *Between the idea*
> *And the reality*
> *Between the motion*
> *And the act*
> *Falls the shadow.*

The white liberal is Augustine praying before his conversion, "Give me chastity and continency, but not yet."

He is Andrew Johnson saying to Negroes in 1864, "I will be your Moses," and taking, in 1865, the posture of Pharaoh.

He is Abraham Lincoln biting his lip, as he put it, and keeping silent.

The white liberal is the man who was not there in Montgomery and Little Rock and Birmingham; the white liberal is the man who is never there. The liberal, as Saul Alinsky, the brilliant white radical said, is the man who leaves the meeting when the fight begins.

It was of the white liberal, or someone like him, that men were thinking when they invented the phrase: he wants to have his cake and to eat it, too. The essential point here is that the white liberal is of no color or race or creed. He is Everyman. "For the good that I would I do not; but the evil which I would not, that I do."

That is it, precisely:

> *Between the desire*
> *And the spasm*
> *Between the potency*
> *And the existence*
> *Between the essence*
> *And the descent*
> *Falls the Shadow.*

The Shadow of safety, the Shadow of comfort, the Shadow of greed, the Shadow of status. This is the white liberal: a man of Shadows, a friend of freedom who pauses, calculates, hesitates.

The dancing waves of revolt and rebellion have exposed with pitiless clarity the dark shadows of the white liberal soul. As a result, the reputation of white liberals in the Negro community is at an all-time low. This is not, as some claim, a perverse spasm of a frustrated folk. The Negro senses dimly that white liberals, despite their failings, are the best America has to offer. And he clings to the white liberal, as a drowning man clings to a plank in a raging sea, not because the plank offers hope of salvation but because it is the very best he has.

The plank is rotten; the sea is choppy—the plank must be made better or we shall all drown.

Let us look closer at the white liberal.

What characterizes the liberal, above all, is his inability to live the words he mouths. The white liberal cannot bear the great white whale of guilt that rises from the sea of Negro degradation and he joins groups and assumes postures that permit him and others to believe something is being done. The key word here is *believe*. The white liberal believes something should be done, but not too soon and not here. He is all negation, the white liberal: now is not the time, this is not the place, the weapon you have is too large or too small. He is all ceremony, all ritual. He pretends, he postures, he resolves. Always, everywhere, in every age, the white liberal flees the principle made black flesh. He wants results without risks, freedom without danger, love without hate. He affirms tomorrow, denies yesterday, and evades today. He is all form, all means, all words—and no substance.

The white liberal is *sui generis*. Men of similar tone and texture exist in South Africa and other countries. But the breed, white liberal, is peculiar to America. No other country has felt called upon to create this office, for it is an office, if not a profession. Lévi-Strauss reminds us that "in any society it is inevitable that a percentage . . . of individuals find themselves placed, as it were, outside of any system or between two or more irreducible systems. The group asks and even requires that these individuals represent certain forms of compromise which cannot be achieved on the collective level, that they simulate imaginary transitions and embody incompatible syntheses."

To "simulate imaginary transitions," to embody incompatible syntheses: this is the function of white liberals. They are ordained to stand in the middle, to sustain hope, to personify an "impossible ideal," and to suffer. They serve the same purpose in the Negro community as token Negroes serve in the white community: they are public monuments of racial progress. In a period of real crisis, white liberals are shoved into the breach between the contending groups to perform four key functions: 1) symbolic flames (tokens of white interest and white good faith); 2) flagellants (whipping boys and deflectors of Negro discontent); 3) channels of communications between separate communities; and 4) expendable platoon leaders of the most advanced positions of the white camp. White liberals are charged, above all, with preventing the coagulation of a massive black clot of Negro discontent. In the March on Washington, it was considered significant that white people participated, thereby preventing an all-Negro demonstration against all white people. In all crises, at all times, white liberals have two basic aims, to prevent polarization and to prevent racial conflict.

Because their aims are so narrow, white liberals are of limited value to Negro leadership. The basic postulates of the white liberal are that bigotry is caused by ignorance and that changes must be carried out quietly, surreptitiously, as it were, so white people will not notice. These assumptions ignore basic considerations of interest and power and permit white liberals to nibble at the edges of the problem without mounting basic assaults on structures of influence and affluence. As Ralph J. Bunche pointed out in the forties, white liberals "are attempting to work within a system which is opposed to any basic change, and they do not try nor do they desire to change that system in any of its fundamentals."

By word and by deed, white liberals insist that Negroes subordinate their claims to the emotions of racists. In the liberal rhetoric, it is considered a provocative act to irritate white racists. It never seems to occur to white liberals that irritated or not they are still the same old racists.

The modern version of this paternalistic theory is that demonstrations enrage white people and imperil the advance of democracy. This statement contains two wholly unacceptable premises. It assumes, first, that white people have some freedom to give and, secondly, that they can dole it out based on the smiles or lack of smiles of the victims. This is a nursery rhyme approach to the historical process and it explains, in part, the continuing distrust of liberals and other white hopes.

White liberals are much given to victim analysis. Nothing pleases the average liberal more than a long and leisurely contemplation of the defects of the victim. The liberal sees quite clearly that the

Negro has been robbed, but in violation of all logic and all law he insists that the robbed instead of the robber make restitution. It is not a pretty picture, this, to see the robber lecturing his victims on the virtues of thrift. Silence were better.

But silence is not the liberal's strong point. Refusing, like practically all other white Americans, to accept Negroes as serious social actors, liberals lecture Negroes on cleanliness, godliness and the duty of obeying laws which white Americans, with white liberal help, have violated for more than one hundred years. Liberals, like practically all other Americans, are paternalistic, patronizing, condescending; they think they can tell Negroes how to frame their posture of protest, how to scream and how to cry or, indeed, whether they should cry at all.

The word *masses* separates Negro activists from Negro militants; the word *conflict* separates white liberals and Negroes. Liberals want orderly change; Negroes want change, orderly if possible, disorderly if necessary. Above all else, the liberal recoils from the shock of conflict. He tends to study much and to pray much. He accepts the goals, but disagrees on the method. The liberal is an aesthete, much preoccupied with form and means and techniques. He looks out on a raging battlefield and sees error everywhere, and he thinks he can find the truth by avoiding error. He is reasonable, the liberal; he preaches and surveys while men are burning churches and rats are biting children.

Prejudice is irrational to its core, but liberals insist that the Negro fight rationally. The Negro is fighting a barroom brawler who knees in the clinches and gouges between rounds; but liberals, standing on the edge of the ring, hold the Negro to *Robert's Rules of Order*.

Moderation: that is the dominant liberal value. Liberals are moderately for the Fourteenth Amendment; they are moderately for Negro freedom, and they think Negroes ought to be moderate. This means almost always that Negroes must dilute their demands, that they must wait, that they must not rock the boat. On every question involving Negro rights, the liberal is moderate—on every question except two: Negro hate and Negro violence. This man, so moderate, so reasonable, so content, becomes an extremist when Negroes hate and hit back. Why? From whence comes this obsession with Negro violence? It stems from an unconscious perception of the ambiguity of the liberal position. Liberals fear Negro violence more than anything else because Negro violence, more than anything else, illuminates the precarious ledge of their posture. White violence, though deplorable, is endurable, and white liberals endure it amazingly well. But Negro violence creates or threatens to create a situation which forces white liberals to choose sides; it exposes their essential support of things as they are.

A dread imperative hangs over the liberal and all other Negro and white Americans—the law of the extreme situation, the dreaded racial conflict that has been predicted every year since the Civil War. It creeps into the dialogue of Negro intellectuals who admit, however reluctantly, that the Black Muslims are, after all, their brothers; it leaps out of the dialogue of liberals who admit, however obliquely, that Richard Russell and George Wallace are, after all, their people.

What the white liberal is saying, always and everywhere, to the Negro, and the Negro to the white liberal, is will you love me in the summer of race riots as you loved me in the spring. And the full horror of our situation is that no man who has not exorcised his own private demons, who has not descended into the lower levels of our very real and menacing collective hell, can stand and look his friend across the line in the eye and say that, God and segregation willing, I will.

As death, the idea of the impossible, shapes and moulds life, so the idea of the impossible in race relations, total confrontation, shapes and moulds the idea of the possible. To choose authentically in the realm of the possible, in life or in race relations, one must choose in the presence of the impossible. As death delimits and defines life, so does total confrontation or its analogue, the race riot, condition and define race relations, not as a reality but as an awful and ever present possibility. No man can live until he exorcises the demons of death; and no man can enter into racial reality until he confronts and transcends the possibility of racial death.

A riot or a situation of heightened hate and tension is a boundary situation that reveals the Negro to himself and the white man to himself. A white liberal, according to the *New York Times*, told a Negro leader that the threatened stall-in at the World's Fair terrified her. "I was more *aware*," she said, "of the fact that I was white and you are Negro."

A boundary situation is a wall, a mirror, in which one sees one's self and the ground of one's being. Not only the white man's face but the white man's soul is reflected in the boundaries between black being and black becoming. It is from this confrontation, it is from his face and also his soul, that the white liberal wants to be protected. He asks the Negro in every possible way to save him from the truth about himself. He says, "Don't push me into a situation, don't create a situation where I will have to say: 'If it comes to that, I choose my people, right or wrong.'"

If it comes to that: this is the categorical imperative of American race relations and it is from this imperative that the white liberal is fleeing. He does not choose; he will not choose and he hates men, he is extreme about men who create situations that force him to choose. To choose what? Not the Negro, but himself. The white liberal is fleeing himself; he is fleeing his own freedom.

When we pass from the white liberal to the mood he personifies we find a similar constriction of vision and purpose. As a retreat from reality, as a distillate of fantasy, as a collection of private phobias, white liberalism is lamed in limb and heart. It is not a philosophy—it is a direction of hope. It is not a movement—it is a fraternity of disturbed souls. It is not a public posture—it is an extended exercise in private evasion.

White liberalism, *a direction of hope* applied to the American race problem, is an extension of Western liberalism and it bears the defects of its birth. The pragmatic biases of Western liberalism lead its adherents to concentrate on the individual to the exclusion of the group, on liberty instead of equality, on gradual rather than precipitous changes.

The defects of this approach in the field of race relations are glaringly apparent. Liberal leadership has no program and when it has a program it deals with symptoms rather than causes. Not knowing what it is for, liberal leadership has not been able to oppose effectively what it is against. It has not prepared the great mass of white people for change. It has not discussed basic issues. White liberalism does not act; it reacts to Negro fury. In fact, one can trace the history of white liberalism by crises in the Negro community. The movement grew out of isolated efforts to reduce racial tensions during World War I and became a going concern during the racial crises of the twenties and the thirties. The Southern Interracial Commission, founded in 1919, was joined by the race relations department of the National Council of Churches during the crucial black nationalist epoch of the twenties. During the thirties, the movement grew apace with the organization of the Catholic Interracial Council and other groups.

Most Negroes, in 1933 and 1963, were openly contemptuous of the programs and policies of the movement which was crisis-inspired and tended to disappear once temperatures in the ghetto dropped to a "normal" level. Conflict-shy, conciliatory, gradualistic, white liberalism tended, in 1933 and 1963 to rely on timid tactics of education, persuasion negotiation. Ralph J. Bunche studied the movement in the late thirties and early forties and concluded that it was made up of a group of "mawkish, missionary-minded sentimentalists" and exceedingly cautious do-gooders.

After the riot season of 1943, white liberalism again bloomed, sprouting forth in hundreds of official and unofficial human relations committees. Most of these committees did nothing; many, in fact, closed shop after the danger of widespread rioting passed. After the collapse of liberal hope in the late forties, the movement entered an interesting phase, which continues today, of *ad hoc* coalition building. Instead of expanding vertically by sending roots down into the Negro and white masses, Negro militants and white liberals decided to expand horizontally by linking civil rights organizations and labor, religious and civil libertarian groups whose roots, on the race issue anyway, were shallow indeed.

The central failure of liberalism, as Myrdal pointed out in 1944—has anyone in America *read* that book—is its failure to develop a mass following. Negro liberals speak often of alliances with white liberals, and it is said rather often nowadays that the future of the Freedom Movement depends on alliances with white liberals. But there has never been an alliance between Negro and white liberal publics, and there cannot be such an alliance because Negro and white liberal publics do not exist. What we have had in the past and what we have today is a *loose alliance between Negro and white liberal leaders*. One needs to be very naive indeed to believe than an alliance between, say, an NAACP leader and the president of the AFL-CIO is anything more than an alliance between two very talented middle-class American men.

What labor leaders, religious leaders and community leaders bring to such an alliance is financial support and letterhead support. But the white liberal leader, whether he represents labor or religion, cannot commit his supporters to a basic racial program and he knows it and Negro leadership knows it. The great mass of laborers, the great mass of Christians, are not ready for a basic and sustained assault on the racial status quo. Why aren't they ready? Because their leaders haven't prepared them, because their leaders don't dare to make an issue of racism in the ranks of organized labor and organized Christianity.

In the final analysis, institutional liberals (labor, religion) are of little value. Racial issues cut across the membership lines of labor and religious organizations and immobilize them when the issue is real and close to home. Few, if any, liberal organizations have enough internal consensus on integrated schools, jobs or housing to be of any value to Negroes in a real fight.

Administrative liberals (social workers, agency executives, et cetera) are hardly more effective. All of them work within a power context controlled by men who are unequivocally opposed to changes in the status quo.

Given this situation, administrative liberals and institutional liberals are reduced to dispensing tea (donations) and sympathy. This, at least, is something; it is a donation if not a down payment on the account of history.

Liberals who join demonstrations, liberals who go up to Harlem to lift up the despairing people, liberals who send letters to Congress: they serve a purpose. But something else is needed, something more basic: the creation of a white liberal public.

The real missionary area in America is not Harlem but White Plains, not the South Side but Evanston. The real missionary area is not the NAACP but the AFL-CIO and the white Christian church. It is there, in the heart of the white liberal camp, that the white liberal must make his last stand.

White liberals cannot convert anyone in America until they convert themselves and their constituencies. The first task of the liberal is the creation of a liberal white public and that public cannot be created except by bare-knuckled fights within the ranks of organized labor and organized Christianity. It is something to send money to Birmingham; but it is more to give Negroes jobs in New York City and to fight for open occupancy in Detroit. It is something to march on a picket line; but it is more to march through the heart of the church.

Let us not deceive ourselves. There is no easy way out. White liberals must stand now, wherever they are, in their offices, in their unions, in their neighborhoods, in their churches, and declare what gods they serve and what visions they have seen.

Some white liberals want change, but almost all white liberals want to achieve it without cost or pain. But it is going to cost. Everybody is going to have to pay something. Our only consolation is that it will cost a great deal more if men decide that they would rather confer now and pay later.

Let us rejoice that it has come to this, that at last, there are no easy ways out and that men's duties lie before them as stark and uncompromising as a cross.

Not until hate becomes as odious to labor as communism.

Not until thousands of churches are emptied, not until thousands of churches are wrecked, not until all churches throw open their doors and invite bigots out.

Not until then.

What holds the liberal back is his essential support of what exists now. White liberals are committed to ways and means and men who are respectable and responsible. But to be responsible to a situation of oppression is, of necessity, to be an oppressor or at least an accomplice of the crime. If defenders of the status quo are permitted to define responsibility and respectability, then men who cling to those values must, of necessity, serve men who make definitions.

What the white liberal lacks is passion. He calls indifference, broad-mindedness; lack of involvement, moderation; disinterest, tolerance. By manipulating approved liberal values, the liberal hides, perhaps even from himself, his basic lack of interest. The cause of the Negro in America would be more than half won if only his friends brought to the battlefield half of the passion of his enemies. If, to be quite precise, white bishops were as impassioned about assassins of the spirit as they are about adulterers, victory would be near. If white men of power hated illicit hate as much as they hate illicit love, it would all be over. If the church loved brotherhood as much as it fears sex, we would now be celebrating the coming of the kingdom of man.

Bigotry flourishes in America because bigotry is respectable. There is no power outside the councils of power that could sustain hate for a moment if it were not sustained inside the councils of power. If freedom is orphaned in America today, it is not because her attackers are strong; it is because men who say they love freedom are timid and passionless and afraid.

It is said often that white liberals are the biggest stumbling block to racial progress in America. There is truth in this, but the truth is of the spirit. White liberals are not the disease; they are symptoms of the disease.

White men of power, with few exceptions, repudiate white liberalism, as timid and ineffective as white liberalism is. Let us be absolutely clear about this: the power structure's program for the Negro community is still Booker T. Washington's program. As a matter of fact, many men of power and many liberals are now convinced that justice for the Negro would destroy the American city.

White men of power are immensely skilled in the use of the ritual phrases of liberalism (without regard to race, creed, et cetera), but they are totally committed to the status quo. What they want—powerful businessmen, prelates, and politicians—from Negro men of power is peace, quiet and pacification of a troubled people. The white power structure, significantly, does not interact with the Negro power structure. Middle men—middle in more ways than one—are delegated to perform the ritual duties of white liberalmanship.

What of the moderates outside the power structure?

Who are they?

"A moderate," Dick Gregory says, "is a cat who will hang you from a low tree." Humor apart, Gregory caught in this definition the fundamental traits of the white moderate, his support of the status quo, his lack of real rancor toward individual Negroes, and also his lack of any real interest.

From the moderate it is but one step to the great uncommitted majority. The first thing we must notice about this group is its nonexistence. The uncommitted majority is a myth spun out of whole cloth by white liberals and moderates who man what Howard N. Meyer, a distinguished white radical, calls the white culture structure. There are no white Americans anywhere who are uncommitted on the issue of race; there are only degrees of hostility. Practically all white Americans believe in white supremacy, and no purpose is served by evading that fact. Because of personal problems and what they believe to be clear and present dangers to their white way of life, some Americans are more vocal and excitable about race. But almost all white Americans support the status quo and the closer the issue comes to home the more obvious their support becomes.

So, we come on the far end of the spectrum to a dead end. Let us go back and weigh the white liberal again. Perhaps he will look better to us now. In truth, the man has his points. He dreams and speaks often of a world where all men would be brothers—if not brothers-in-law. He believes, with varying degrees of sincerity, in the necessity of gradual moves toward our national purpose. Since the white liberal, when compared with the moderate and the racist and the great uncommitted hostility, is such a decent chap, why is he being attacked. Because he stands on the same platform as the white supremacist, because he has a line in his office or in his neighborhood, not to pursue the matter further, beyond which he is not willing for Negroes to go. Let us come to this point and stand on it: here the air is clear and cold, and the dangers great. The white liberal and the white supremacist share the same root postulates. They are different in degree, not kind. And while we ought to thank God for small favors we are under no obligation to call a horse chestnut a chestnut horse, as Abraham Lincoln said of his racial posture.

Both Negro strategy and racist strategy are based on the same intelligence, the perception of the ambiguity of the white liberal. Liberals are attacked in the ghetto because Negroes perceive dimly that if liberals cannot be driven from the ranks of white supremacy, then all, literally all, is lost.

Liberals are defined at the wall by their hidden (often from themselves) emotional ties to the status quo. At the point of blood—metaphorically in amalgamation; physically in interracial conflict; symbolically in positions of real power for Negro males —*at the point of blood*, the liberal draws back. He is a being defined by subordination to a triad of blood.

No one knows this better than the racist. Racist strategy is based on the belief that if you push a white liberal against the wall, *that if you scratch him*, you will find a racist. That strategy, incidentally, is based on good psychology and we must note that it has not failed in a single crisis situation since the Civil War. There are no degrees of racism, as Thurgood Marshall used to say. One cannot be a little bit pregnant.

Anyone who doubts this need only look around him. The whole face of America yields abundant testimony of the unreliability of white liberals. In fact, the unreliability of the liberal is inversely proportional to the amount of danger the Negro faces. When the danger is greatest, when the Negro needs white liberals most, they are nowhere to be found.

Liberals, moreover, have found it necessary to make repeated sacrifices of the Negro on the altar of national unity. When, after Reconstruction, it was necessary to throw Negroes overboard to reconcile the North and South, liberal journals and old abolitionists led the cheering section. It has happened over and over again and, for all we know, it may happen again.

Bad faith—the history of white liberalism is a history of bad faith. It is also, to be sure, a history of good intentions. But hell and segregation being what they are, let us not speak of good intentions.

The deep and very real hostility between Negroes and white liberals stems from a deep and very real fact: betrayal. By using Negroes as *occasions* for demonstrations of tolerance and *objects* for expiation of guilt, by leading Negroes on to hope and then betraying them, white liberals have played a major role in magnifying Negro cynicism and despair.

For a great many years, Negroes ignored or pretended to ignore the mote in their friend's eye. But for several years now a special intensity of hatred has been building up in the ghetto against all white liberals.

The problem, broadly stated, is that liberals, like practically all Americans, find it difficult to respond to Negroes as human beings. They either see the Negro as a victim or a problem or a statistic, anything and everything except a live, palpitating human being.

It has always been hard for liberals to practice what they preach. The Quakers, the dear, mild, God-intoxicated Quakers, loved Negroes, generally speaking, best when they were farthest away. The Quakers started the antislavery campaign, but there was a place for Negroes in their world view and special benches for them in their meeting houses.

One of the most distressing facets of the antislavery movement was the inability of so many abolitionists to go beyond reform and recognize Negroes as human beings. Paradoxically, it was easier for most abolitionists to die for the Negro than to live with him. It was a very modern failing, this. Sarah Douglass found the Jim Crow benches in the Quaker meeting houses intolerable. "I like their principles," she said, "but not their practices," adding: "Many, very many are anxious to take up the cross, but how few are strong enough to bear it."

In 1847, William Wells Brown, the Negro abolitionist, said what Adam Clayton Powell said in 1963: "Save me from my friends"—I know, understand, and can handle my enemies. I have *named* them; I have them under control.

The white abolitionists of whom Brown spoke neither hired Negro workers nor heeded the voices of Negro leaders. Nor did their sons and daughters. It is not without a certain significance that most of the great white philanthropists found Booker T. Washington more congenial than W. E. B. Du Bois. Julius Rosenwald was a metaphor of the age of philanthropy. He gave millions of dollars to poor, unfortunate Negroes but he refused to institute a fair hiring policy at Sears and Roebuck's. Somehow, it has always been easier for the Negro's friends to give him doles instead of justice. All the money given to Negroes by all the philanthropists in the history of America would not equal the amount diverted from Negroes in one year because of their color.

Separated by words and attitudes and lies, Negroes and white liberals have fought, almost constantly, over the lines of leadership. Since Frederick Douglass contested William Lloyd Garrison's right to speak for Negroes, there has been no end of controversy. The early NAACP was almost wrecked by a series of internal civil wars between W. E. B. Du Bois and the ruling white liberal elite. Things reached such a pass that Du Bois, probably with tongue in cheek, suggested the establishment of sep-

arate but equal divisions of the National Association for the Advancement of Colored People.

It would be a mistake to view all this as the do-
ings of wicked white men. We are not, to repeat,
talking about evil men; we are talking about good
men who did not or could not flesh out their goodness. We are talking, in short, about tragedy, not
villainy. The tragedy of the white liberal is his
situation and the situation of the Negro victim.
What vitiates the Negro-white dialogue at its roots
is a situation of oppression and injustice. And it is
impossible to be just in a situation of injustice. One
can be kind, perhaps, or even charitable; but
neither kindliness nor charity is justice. A colonial
cannot deal justly with a native, nor can a *white*
man deal justly with a Negro. What is required is
for the oppressor to cease to be an oppressor, for
the colonial to cease being a colonial and the white
man to cease being a *white* man. A white man, so
long as he clings to the privileges and prerogatives
of a white man, so long as he identifies with a system of oppression which includes the Negro as a
victim, cannot interact in any meaningful way with
a Negro. Nor, to be sure, can a Negro interact with
a white man so long as he remains within the bounds
of the given, so long, in fact, as he accepts the
definitions and values of his oppressors, so long as
he admits, in short, that he is a Negro and that *that*
is something shameful.

Before there can be real dialogue, the situation
must be smashed or at least transcended. A situation of oppression destroys the only ground on
which dialogue can be founded, mutuality and reci-

procity. So long as the situation remains whole, suspicion, hostility and distrust will remain whole.

Moreover, the logic of the situation demands of white men an act of which most men are incapable, a repudiation of themselves and a reconstruction of themselves. It creates a climate in which the white liberal, in order to be authentic, must be for the destruction of himself insofar as he remains, even symbolically, an oppressor.

To rise above the situation, to transcend it, to impose on it new levels of meaning and significance: this is a private solution available to marginal individuals on the margins of the culture. But it is a private solution, and private enclaves are terribly vulnerable as long as the situation of oppression remains whole and individuals retain roots in the mutually exclusive worlds of the oppressed and the oppressor.

It was to this situation that Richard Wright addressed himself in *Native Son*. With chilling insight, Wright made Bigger kill not a racist but an avowed friend. Mary Dalton, the blonde, blue-eyed object of Bigger's hate as well as his desire, was a left-winger devoted to Negro causes and her father was a millionaire who had given millions of dollars to Negro colleges—millions of dollars, Wright noted acidly, that came, in part, from the exploitation of Negroes.

In an odd reversal of the golden rule, Bigger hated Mary Dalton and her boyfriend, Jan, as he hated himself. He hated them because they "looked" at him, because in their eyes he saw himself and he was undone, because kindness, charity, tea and sympathy were irrelevant to his situation, because they—white people—had inflicted the wound from which he suffered and it was insulting for them to come to him and to ask him to describe his pains.

Life betrayed Bigger and Mary Dalton. She took Bigger's hand to prove that she had no prejudice, and she reminded him, unbearably, of the thousands on thousands of black men who died because white women lived. She got in the front seat of the car and she reminded Bigger of the back seat.

What we must notice here is that Mary Dalton was not doing what she thought she was doing. There are no pure social acts. Acts to be meaningful must body forth from a shared tradition. And the only tradition that Bigger and Mary Dalton shared was a tradition of horror.

With the context of that tradition, Mary was free to seek Bigger out and to be kind. But, alas, Bigger did not have the same freedom. He could not go to her and hold her hand and ask her to take him to one of those little places where her people ate.

By flaunting her freedom, Mary, inevitably, reminded Bigger of his lack of freedom. She was pure choice, pure project, pure freedom; he was all passivity, all object, all slavery. The only place he could re-establish reciprocity and communication and humanity was hate. And, of course, he hated her, not knowing why. His choice, given Mary Dalton's good will, was tragic. But how could it be otherwise, since the situation in which Mary Dalton and Bigger Thomas were enwebbed was tragic.

This was, to be sure, an extreme situation, but it

is from extreme situations that we must start, or we shall all end in an extreme situation. In order for Negroes and white liberals to communicate they must break out of the glass cage of caste and hate that contains them. Negroes have a duty to assimilate their situation, to accept it and transmute it so they can view white liberal approaches with greater objectivity. But the power and the glory are the white man's; and so is the responsibility. An act to the end is a minimum requirement. Anything else is silence, evasion, and untruth. The Negro hates his role in America and he hates white liberals who approach him in the aspect of *white* liberals and remind him, however obliquely, of his situation. For white people to pretend surprise at this fact is not only naive but downright cynical. And to pretend, as many do, that Negro hate is of the same tone and texture as white hate is ludicrous. As Arnold Rose pointed out—and I use Rose because he is a perceptive non-Negro—"[Negro] hatred of white people is not pathological—far from it. It is a healthy human reaction to oppression, insult, and terror. White people are often surprised at the Negro's hatred of them, but it should not be surprising.

"The whole world knows that the Nazis murdered millions of Jews and can suspect that the remaining Jews are having some emotional reaction to that fact. Negroes, on the other hand, are either ignored or thought to be so subhuman that they have no feelings when one of their number is killed because he was a Negro. Probably no week goes by in the United States that some Negro is not severely beaten, and the news is reported in the Negro press. Every week or maybe twice a week almost the entire Negro population of the United States suffers an emotional recoil from some insult coming from the voice or pen of a leading white man. The surviving Jews had one, big, soul-wracking 'incident' that wrenched them back to group identification. The surviving Negroes experience constant jolts that almost never let them forget for even an hour that they are Negroes. In this situation, hatred of whites and group identification are natural reactions."

There are hundreds of ways of hating the white man in America, including imitating him. But the harsh fact is that the choice for most Negroes is not between hating or loving but between hating and hating, between hating themselves or hating their oppressors.

This should surprise no literate man. You cannot deny people the basic emotions of rage, resentment and, yes, hate. Only slaves or saints or masochists love their oppressors. If you humiliate a man, if you degrade him, if you do this over and over for hundreds of years, he will either hate you or hate himself. This is a basic fact of humanity, and Negroes are human. At best, you will get that strange kind of love Camus spoke of—the love of Jesus and Gandhi, a love that expresses itself in creative resentment, in the cursing of fig trees and the driving of money changers from temples.

A strange kind of love or a strange kind of hate.

Martin Luther King, Jr., or Malcolm X.

Either/or.

It would help enormously in America if there

were a ten-year moratorium on the use of the word love. Love and hate are not mutually exclusive phenomena; they are two sides of the same coin and they are found almost always in different degrees in the same relation. The Negro loves white Americans but he also hates white Americans and there is nothing that can be done about it until the white liberal addresses himself to conditions that breed love, hate, and desperation. It is not required, finally, that we love each other. What is required is something infinitely more difficult, for us to confront each other.

But this is what the white liberal refuses to do. The white liberal is fleeing the truth of his, of *our* situation. He is seeking personal salvation not justice. He is moved not only by a vision of the future but by a horror of the past, not by the Negro, but by himself. What moves him is guilt. What the liberal seeks is his lost innocence. What the liberal wants, paradoxically, is for the Negro to tell him that he is not as white and as cold as snow.

The key to an understanding of the white liberal is that he is fleeing a situation of horror and its self-enforcing sentence of deceit. It is from the Negro situation that he wants to be protected. He seeks out words and Negroes who will tell him that the situation does not exist. And since the Talented Tenth, with whom white liberals interact, are fleeing the same situation, liberals find what they seek. Since white liberals and the Talented Tenth say the situation does not exist, they cannot make a meaningful comment on it. Because they deny reality, they cannot shape reality. Fleeing truth, they lose the power to make the truth.

The basic, the indispensable, the crucial deceit of liberalism is that nobody has been hurt. A few scratches perhaps or a bruise or two, but nothing requiring radical surgery. If white liberals confronted the Negro-white situation in its totality of horror, they would perforce move forward into radical action or collapse in a moral spasm.

If white men who call themselves liberals do not recognize themselves in this assessment, then they are not liberals. They may be something less or, hopefully, something more.

Programmatically, pragmatically and spiritually, the white liberal is totally inadequate to the demands of the hour. In order to do now what must be done, the white liberal must become not liberal but relevant which is only to say that he must become radical.

At all times and in all climes, Negroes have worked best with radicals. It oftentimes happens that a white radical—a Garrison, for example—will prepare the ground for a white liberal or a moderate—a Lincoln, for example. But historically and spiritually, the white radical comes first. And who is a white radical? A man who confronts radical problems and articulates radical solutions, a man who transcends we-groups and out-groups, whose loyalties are to a group beyond groups, a man whose kingdom, so to speak, is not of this world—a man, in short, who is free.

Negroes usually find their most reliable allies among men who have broken in some way with the dominant myths of the age. Rarely, if ever, are reliable allies found in the camp of the conventional.

Judged by past experiences, radicalism, the indigenous, noncommunist radicalism of a Paine or a Darrow or a Phillips, is the minimum hope of the Negro. Men who have become radicals, men who have, at least, repudiated liberalism, are often ideal advocates of the cause of the oppressed. Such men, because of their marginality and objectivity, are sometimes better friends of the oppressed than the oppressed.

Indigenous radicals speak to America from the much-maligned tradition of Thomas Paine, Wendell Phillips, John Brown, Frederick Douglass, Clarence Darrow and Saul Alinsky. It is to this tradition that we must go for hope. And it is to this tradition that white men of good will must repair if hope is to become more than a palliative.

White radicals, whatever their personal limitations, construct acts to the end. They do not shrink from conflict or combat. Like Jesus, like Toussaint, like Paine, like every radical in the history of man, they take the vow of poverty, forsaking, if necessary, all others. Wendell Phillips, the Boston patrician, abandoned place and position for the slave. So enamored was he of Negro freedom that his family tried unsuccessfully to commit him to an insane asylum.

Flowing out of the radical tradition is a sense of real repentance and shame and a repudiation of the pride and pretensions of men with white skins. "I never rise to address a colored audience," William L. Garrison said, "without feeling ashamed of my color; ashamed of being identified with a race of men who have done you so much injustice and yet retain so large a portion of your brethren in servitude."

Empathy: it is this that divides radicals and liberals. Radicals suffer with the oppressed. They feel the blows, they weep, they hunger, they thirst. Because they project themselves into the situation of oppression, radicals are not tolerant of men who sustain situations of oppression. They focus their fire on good people. They try in words that are "half battles," to quote Wendell Phillips, to force good people to recognize their complicity in systems of evil. Radicals stand with Burke who said that to speak of atrocious crimes in mild language is treason to virtue," with Jesus who found, that love and gentility apart, it was sometimes necessary to *name* evil, to speak of "fools," "hypocrites," "devourers of widows' houses," "serpents" and "generation of vipers."

The law of relevance and of radicalism finds focus in the lives of two men who symbolize, above all other Americans, the polar qualities of white liberals and white radicals. The first man, Abraham Lincoln, is, of course, the godfather of American liberalism. It is to him, or rather to his image, that white liberals go for sustenance and support. From a historical standpoint, the choice of Lincoln was unfortunate. Lincoln was neither a racial liberal nor a moderate; he was a conservative who, nonetheless, personified in his groping and his vacillations the limitations of the liberal mood. Although the Illinois of his day was a government of the white people, for the white people, and by the white people, Lincoln made no audible protest. In fact, at Charleston, Illinois, on September 18, 1858, during the Lincoln-Douglas debates, he said he preferred it that way. "I am not, nor ever have been in favor of bringing about in any way the social and political equality of the white and black races; I am not nor ever have been in favor of making voters of the free Negroes, or jurors, or qualifying them to hold office, or having them marry with white people. I will say in addition that there is a physical difference between the white and black races which, I suppose, will forever forbid the two races living together upon terms of social and political equality; and inasmuch as they cannot so live, that while they do remain together, there must be the position of the superiors and the inferiors; and that I, as much as any other man, am in favor of the superior being assigned to the white man."

Lincoln's verbal dexterity befuddled his opponent, Stephen Douglas. Lincoln was given to stating in the same speech that he believed in white supremacy and the *principle* of the Declaration of Independence. Douglas could never understand why the crowd applauded Lincoln at both points. His inability to grasp the fact that white Americans believed and believe in both—white supremacy and the Declaration of Independence—probably cost him the Presidency.

Lincoln went his way, endorsing both white supremacy and the Declaration of Independence and refusing to take a stand on the issue of Negro rights in Illinois. His approach to the racial problem, he said once, was to bite his lips and keep silent. In that image is the whole history of white liberalism in America.

As President, Lincoln was scrupulously correct, stating the principle with great eloquence and avoiding rigid commitments to the practice. He was in favor of a gradual emancipation program extending to the year 1900 and the deportation, if possible, of Negro freedmen. It was his opinion that Negro and white Americans would be a great deal better off if they were separated, preferably with a very large body of water between them.

Lincoln grew during the war, but he did not grow much on the racial issue. On the eve of his death, he was ready to bless a Reconstruction program for Louisiana that was very charitable to ex-slaveholders and exceedingly cruel to freedmen and Negro soldiers who, he admitted, had helped to win the war. He barely suggested privately that it would perhaps be a good thing if the white men of Louisiana would give the vote to "very intelligent" Negroes and Negro veterans. "Barely suggested," "privately," "very intelligent Negroes," "perhaps"—thus speaks the liberal or the moderate in a direct confrontation of Negro rights and white interests.

To Lincoln, the Union was more dear than freedom. To the abolitionists, freedom was more dear than the Union. The white students and white adults who have taken up the real burden of the white man in the ranks of the Negro Freedom Movement are made in the image of the white abolitionists—Garrison, Phillips, Charles Sumner and Thaddeus Stevens—who were largely responsible for forcing the issue of Negro freedom that Lincoln and other liberals and moderates were trying to evade. In the Civil War and the post-Civil War period, these men made a determined effort to flesh out the American creed and America has never forgiven them. The continual villification of the abolitionists indicates that America is still not ready to face the problems they faced. The continual glorification of the conservative Lincoln indicates that America is still trying to evade the problem Lincoln tried to evade.

Not only white but Negro Americans, many of whom know better, sing the strange chorus of Lincoln and moderation. For men, Negro and white, who dread the hard claims of responsibility and the duty of claiming their freedom and validating it day by day, Lincoln is an image of evasion. In Lincoln, white Americans see themselves giving freedom, and since freedom is given by a stroke of the pen, it is not necessary for anyone to do anything. Lincoln, disengaged from Garrison, Frederick Douglass, John Brown and the men, black and white, who died in the Civil War, is a figure of pure fantasy and irrelevancy. It is Hollywood enshrined in history and history sucked of all possible meaning and content. Freedom is not and cannot be given. There is no racial Santa Claus. There is no great white father in the sky who gives out freedom out of the goodness of his heart on January 1.

Because of his undoubted largeness of character, because, when pushed against the wall, he rose to the occasion, Lincoln is dear to Americans. But so, if life has any meaning, is truth; and it was to truth that Frederick Douglass addressed himself when he rose in 1876 to eulogize Lincoln before an audience that included President Grant, members of the Supreme Court and other dignitaries. "It must be admitted," Douglass said, "truth compels me to admit, even here in the presence of the monument we have erected to his memory, Abraham Lincoln was not, in the fullest sense of the word, either our man or our model. In his interests, in his associations, in his habits of thought, and in his prejudices, he was a white man. He was pre-eminently the white man's President, entirely devoted to the welfare of white men."

Lincoln's interests were not John Brown's interests, and it is to John Brown that we must go, finally, if we want to understand the limitations and the possibilities of our situation. He was of no color, John Brown, of no race or age. He was pure passion, pure transcendence. He was an elemental force like the wind, rain and fire. "A volcano beneath a mountain of snow," someone called him.

A great gaunt man with a noble head, the look of a hawk and the intensity of a saint, John Brown lived and breathed justice. As a New England businessman, he sacrificed business and profits, using his warehouse as a station on the Underground Railroad. In the fifties, he became a full-time friend of freedom, fighting small wars in Kansas and leading a group of Negro slaves out of Missouri. Always, everywhere, John Brown was preaching the primacy of the act. "Slavery is evil," he said, "kill it."

"But we must study the problem . . ."
Slavery is evil—kill it!
"We will hold a conference . . ."
Slavery is evil—kill it!
"But our allies . . ."
Slavery is evil—kill it!

John Brown was contemptuous of conferences and study groups and graphs. "Talk, talk, talk," he said. Women were suffering, children were dying—and grown men were talking. Slavery was not a word; it was a fact, a chain, a whip, an event; and it seemed axiomatic to John Brown that facts could only be contraverted by facts, a life by a life.

There was in John Brown a complete identification with the oppressed. It was his child that a slaveowner was selling; his sister who was being whipped in the field; his wife who was being raped in the gin house. It was not happening to Negroes; it was happening to him. Thus it was said that he could not bear to hear the word slave spoken. At the sound of the word, his body vibrated like the strings of a sensitive violin. John Brown *was* a Negro, and it was in this aspect that he suffered.

More than Frederick Douglass, more than any other Negro leader, John Brown suffered with the slave. "His zeal in the cause of freedom," Frederick Douglass said, "was infinitely superior to mine. Mine was as the taper light; his was as the burning sun. Mine was bounded by time; his stretched away to the silent shores of eternity. I could speak for the slave; John Brown could fight for the slave. I could live for the slave; John Brown could die for the slave."

In the end, John Brown made of himself an act of transcendence. The act he chose—the tools, the means, the instruments—does not concern us here. His act, as it happened, was violent and apocalyptic; but it could have been as gentle as rain in the spring, a word perhaps, yes, or a name or a life committed to a piece of paper. Acts to the end grow out of the lineaments of men's lives and it is up to each man to create and invent not only his act but also the occasion of his act.

John Brown made his occasion, attacking the arsenal at Harpers Ferry in the hope of creating a situation in which slaves all over the South would flock to him. He begged his old friend, Frederick Douglass, to accompany him; but Douglass insisted that the plan was premature. The old white man and the young Negro argued from eight one night to three the next morning. While they argued, a tough cynical fugitive slave named Shields Green watched and weighed. After the argument, Douglass rose and asked Shields Green if he were ready to go. Green thought for a moment and then said: "I believe I go wid de old man." Shields Green was in the mountains and could have escaped when federal troops closed in on John Brown. A man suggested flight, but Shields Green said: "I believe I go down wid de old man." And he did—all the way to the gallows.

Why did Green deliberately sacrifice his life?

Not because he was irrevocably committed to John Brown's way but because he was irrevocably committed to John Brown, because, in a horribly bloody and horribly tangible way, a prayer had been answered; because he had at long last found a man, neither black nor white, who was willing to go all the way.

Who?

"I believe I go wid de old man."

Who?

"A man for all seasons," a pillar of fire by night and a cloud by day.

Who?

A John Brown or a Wendell Phillips or a Paine. It may be that America can no longer produce such men. If so, all is lost. Cursed is the nation, cursed is the people, who can no longer breed indigenous radicals when it needs them.

There was an America once that was big enough for a Wendell Phillips; there was even an America big enough for a Brown.

What happened to that America?

Who killed it?

We killed it, all of us, Negroes and whites, with our petty evasions and paternalistic doles, with our sycophantic simpering and our frantic flights from truth and risk and danger. We killed it, all of us, liberals and activists with the rest. Can the stone be rolled once again from the mouth of the cave? It is my faith—and all Negroes who do not have that faith are in or on their way to prisons, asylums or Paris—that buried somewhere deep beneath the detergents and lies is the dead body of the America that made Thomas Jefferson a lawbreaker and John Brown a martyr.

Can the stone be rolled away again?

Few American white men when sufficiently drunk

can resist the temptations of toying with that mad idea. They come, martinis in hand, faces flushed, guilt waving, and they say: "There was this bright little old Negro boy in my class and I wonder what happened to him." Or, since speculations about the fate of bright black boys are dangerous, "There was this little old Negro girl." They say, oh, so many things and it doesn't matter for they are not saying what they are saying. What this man or that man is saying, really, is that, "I am ashamed of myself." He is saying, "There is something deep within me." He is saying, "I am better than I am."

He may be; but saying will not make it so.

"There was this little old Negro boy . . ."

Segregation is evil—kill it!

"We will hold a conference . . ."

Segregation is evil—kill it!

"But our allies . . ."

Segregation is evil—kill it!

For the Jew in Germany, the African in Salisbury, the Negro in New York:

Who?

A man beyond good and evil, beyond tea and sympathy, beyond black and white.

Who?

"A man for all seasons," a pillar of fire by night and a cloud by day.

Who?

"I believe I go down wid de old man."

About the Author

LERONE BENNETT, JR., is the author of *Before the Mayflower: A History of the Negro in America, 1619-1962,* which was one of the most widely acclaimed popular treatments of Negro history in the past decade. A social historian, he has expressed candid views on the present state of race relations that have won for him wide recognition both as a writer and as a lecturer. His poems, short stories, and articles have appeared in the pages of many periodicals, and he has published a biography of Martin Luther King, Jr., *What Manner of Man,* in 1965. A native of Clarksdale, Mississippi, and a graduate of Morehouse College in Atlanta, Georgia, Mr. Bennett now lives in Chicago with his wife and four children. He is Senior Editor of *Ebony* Magazine.